DANGERS MEN FACE

Overcoming the Five Greatest Threats to Living Life Well

J E R R Y   W H I T E

To [handwritten] ____

For a life of wealthy through these Dangers. Prov 22:3

[signature]
8 Feb 02

NAVPRESS ●

BRINGING TRUTH TO LIFE
NavPress Publishing Group
P.O. Box 35001, Colorado Springs, Colorado 80935

248·842
whi

The Navigators is an international Christian organization. Our mission is to reach, disciple, and equip people to know Christ and to make Him known through successive generations. We envision multitudes of diverse people in the United States and every other nation who have a passionate love for Christ, live a lifestyle of sharing Christ's love, and multiply spiritual laborers among those without Christ.

NavPress is the publishing ministry of The Navigators. NavPress publications help believers learn biblical truth and apply what they learn to their lives and ministries. Our mission is to stimulate spiritual formation among our readers.

© 1997 by Jerry E. White
Library of Congress Catalog Card Number: 97-8895
ISBN 1-57683-005-5

Cover illustration: Linda Chesak/The Stock Illustration

Some of the anecdotal illustrations in this book are true to life and are included with the permission of the persons involved. All other illustrations are composites of real situations, and any resemblance to people living or dead is coincidental.

Unless otherwise identified, all Scripture quotations in this publication are taken from the *HOLY BIBLE: NEW INTERNATIONAL VERSION* ® (NIV®). Copyright © 1973, 1978, 1984 by International Bible Society. Used by permission of Zondervan Publishing House. All rights reserved. Other versions used include: the *New American Standard Bible* (NASB), © The Lockman Foundation 1960, 1962, 1963, 1968, 1971, 1972, 1973, 1975, 1977; *The Message: New Testament with Psalms and Proverbs* by Eugene H. Peterson, copyright © 1993, 1994, 1995, used by permission of NavPress Publishing Group; *The Living Bible* (TLB), copyright © 1971, used by permission of Tyndale House Publishers, Inc., Wheaton, IL 60189, all rights reserved; and the *King James Version* (KJV).

White, Jerry E., 1937–
    Dangers men face : overcoming the five greatest threats to living life well / by Jerry White.
        p.   cm.
    ISBN 1-57683-005-5 (pbk.)
    1. Men—Religious life. 2. Men—Conduct of life. I. Title.
BV4528.2.W47   1997
248.8'42—dc21   97-8895
                                                                  CIP

Printed in the United States of America

2 3 4 5 6 7 8 9 10 11 12 13 14 15 / 00 99

CONTENTS

Dedicated to the memory of our son
Stephen Jerry White
1959–1990

His life and his death
have caused me to reflect more deeply
on all the dangers
described in this book.

Foreword
and Acknowledgments

Every book has a history. *Dangers Men Face* has been especially long and somewhat agonizing in its journey from mind and heart to ink and paper. It began with a small meeting of Navigator men in New Zealand as I shared some dangers they would likely face in their lives. Their response and interaction caused me to develop the subject more thoroughly. So thanks to each of those Kiwi friends!

The birth of this book was complicated even more by the untimely death of my son. Such an event drained emotional strength to such an extent that energy and motivation for writing were often squeezed out by the demands of my work as president of The Navigators and by the incessant changes taking place in my own life. In the meantime, many have contributed to my thinking on these topics. Chris Canlis, Doug Hignell, and Stan Newell have kept me accountable on many areas mentioned. My wife, Mary, continued to encourage and edit even as she worked on her book *Harsh Grief, Gentle Hope*. Mary has been my collaborator and friend through these years which have been difficult for both of us. She sees similar patterns for women.

My thanks to Steve Webb, Lori Mitchell, Tim Howard, Denise Foerch, and the rest of the team at NavPress as they edited, challenged, and clarified my thinking and expression. Thanks also to my assistant Adam Holz who helped me with many of the discussion questions.

The final result has been influenced by many, but the responsibility for all that is written is mine. The illustrations are real, though some are composites. Except in a few obvious instances, names and precise circumstances have been changed to protect people's privacy. These ideas are not theoretical. They are real, having been forged in the crucible of my own life and molded by the Scriptures and my friends.

Reading this book is only a start. I encourage you to interact over it with a small group of men. That will be key to moving from ideas and thoughts to life and action.

Dr. Jerry White
Colorado Springs
February 1997

A Dangerous Journey

CHAPTER ONE

A DANGEROUS JOURNEY

Every man wants to finish life well. No man sets out early in his life to destroy himself. He doesn't plan to strike up failure after failure. He does not get married intending to make himself and his wife miserable. He does not plan to be a poor father. He does not coldly calculate how he will become an alcoholic and ruin his liver by age forty. But the journey is filled with danger. Finishing well is a tremendous challenge.

At the beginning a man envisions a life of fulfillment and at least moderate success. He dreams of a lovely wife and family, living in a comfortable home. He plans to take his daughter to gymnastics and his son to little league baseball. He imagines a stable job and financial success. He sees himself happily walking down the aisle at his daughter's wedding. He envisions fishing with his grandchildren and spoiling them on birthdays and holidays.

Few men write out these dreams. But they are there, as present as the sunrise, as compelling as a smile from a beautiful woman — especially the one he hopes will be his wife. Dreams are often unspoken, but always in the recesses of his mind. Just as a young boy fantasizes about being a star football player or a professional baseball player, so every man fantasizes about his future.

A man's picture of his future gradually evolves as he grows up. He observes his father with his foibles and his successes. Or he sees many fathers in the serial marriage scene. His idealistic picture develops a few cracks. He does not want to be like that. He sees role models of teachers, neighbors, coaches. Most young men have little discernment as to the quality of these role models. But something inside him picks the best of them all and creates the dream — absent of trouble and full of happiness.

> *Something inside him picks the best of them all and creates the dream — absent of trouble and full of happiness.*

A friend recently sent me a picture taken when I was eleven. I stared at a blond, smiling, shy young boy who had no idea what was ahead. Even at that innocent age, I remember the beginning of fears that life was not all that it was cracked up to be. Yet my life was an empty pad of paper waiting for a story to be written upon it.

As a man embarks on the teen years and young adulthood, the cold reality of life begins to sober him. The idyllic road is not so smooth after all. There are bumps and potholes, detours and dead ends, hills and valleys. It is a road filled with dangers at every turn — some under our control, but many that come upon us like a sudden afternoon thunderstorm.

The word "danger" brings a variety of mind pictures to every man, depending on his experience. Some remember the near miss at an intersection while driving. Others remember escaping a terrible accident with only minor injuries in spite of a totally wrecked car. Some think of children playing too close to a precipice in the mountains or near a busy street. Some recall a child not coming home from school on time, causing a frantic search and the fear of abduction. Some may recall terrifying incidents of abuse and mistreatment. Others fear having no money or job.

Each of these dangers is real. Any one of them could happen. *But the dangers we need to fear the most are the ones we do not see until it is too late.* It is like traveling in a country where cars drive on the opposite side of the road. As pedestrians, all our instincts tell us to look in the wrong direction for traffic. Many times when traveling I have been restrained by a friend who knew I would make that mistake. They protected me from getting hit. Danger is like a cancer that grows within us, unknown until it sinks roots of death into our bodies. Danger is like the cholesterol clogging our arteries, building silently until we have a heart attack.

It is the unexpected dangers, those that are silent and subtle. . . . They are spiritual and practical issues which I believe every man faces almost daily— but which have such a silent appeal that they slide by unnoticed.

It is the unexpected dangers, those that are silent and subtle, that I will address in the next chapters. They are spiritual and practical issues which I believe every man faces almost daily—but which have such a silent appeal that they slide by unnoticed. The effects of these dangers dull our spiritual lives, cripple our effectiveness and happiness, and generally turn us from a vital walk with God. And as a natural corollary, they poison relationships with our wives, children, and friends.

Even for a committed believer in Christ, these dangers are always present. Not just casual believers or halfhearted believers are at risk. Most of us believe that "Satan walks about seeking whom he can devour." This is true, but it also takes a more sinister form, "Satan sneaks about seeking whom he can entice and coax into the first delicious steps of seemingly harmless indiscretion."

In these few short chapters, I would like to share from my experience, and from the Scriptures, *five dangers* which have the potential to destroy a man just as cancer destroys the body. These dangers vary from subtle to blatant, avoidable to unavoidable, constant to intermittent. I have seen these primary dangers in my own life and in the lives of others. A great danger for one man may be minor for another. We are all different and respond differently to circumstances and events. But, to some extent, we face all five dangers at some point in our lives.

It would be totally unfair to simply throw up danger signs without some other signs telling you where to turn—instructions on how to drive through or detour around the danger zone. With each danger I have attempted to identify one or two key biblical concepts as antidotes and preventatives. Profound fundamental truths undergird much of what I share. These truths include God's grace, God's sovereignty, the nature of salvation, the person and work of Christ, the pervasiveness of sin, the nature of man, and the place of good works. These are important biblical concepts which rightfully warrant far more than I will write here. I will often refer to one of these basic tenants of life in Christ. I leave it to you to pursue them further, depending on where you are in your spiritual pilgrimage.

Walk with me now through these five danger zones.

QUESTIONS FOR THOUGHT AND DISCUSSION

1. What are your dreams? How have they changed over the years?

2. Are some dangers, by nature, more subtle and less easily detected than others? If so, give an example.

3. Describe one change that crept up on you unexpectedly.

THE DANGER OF LOSS

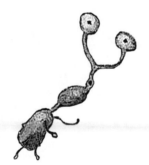

CHAPTER TWO

THE DANGER OF LOSS

I REMEMBER the first time that I experienced a deep sense of loss. It occurred early one cold January morning in 1946. At age eight I climbed into a car with my mother and my new stepfather. We said tearful goodbyes and drove out of the tiny town of Garden City, Iowa, heading to an unknown future in the state of Washington. I left my grandfather behind; he had become my surrogate father following my parents' divorce when I was a few months old. I loved him dearly, depended on him, found my security in him. And now I was losing him—for what I thought was forever. Promises of letters do not mean much to an eight year old. And in that day and age, long-distance phone calls were virtually unheard of for ordinary people.

That was a terrible loss for me. It took me years to recover. Later

I would be so lonely in that "metropolis" of 180,000 people in Spokane, Washington, that the only solution was to send me back to Iowa to visit. For several years I made a summer trek to be with my grandfather. He was a widower so we "batched" together. I was trying to recover some of what I had lost. My stepfather back in Spokane was a fine person, but he was not "Grandpa Tony."

That loss marked me for life, probably in ways I will never know. Every human being must grapple with the reality of loss. From our earliest years we experience the joys of gain and the agony of loss. Loss is one of the basic building blocks of maturity.

Some losses are open wounds, clearly seen and painful. Others are silent, unknown except for their pervasive effect on our current and later lives. How much did my parents' divorce affect me? I did not sense any loss in my emotions, since I was a baby. Yet it was a real loss with real consequences. Thousands of children growing up with only one parent feel the same loss. The divorce deeply moved my mother, affecting her emotional state for many years to come, thus influencing me in subtle ways.

> *Every human being must grapple with the reality of loss.*

In retrospect I can more fully understand her anxieties and responses in our home and toward my stepfather. They had a wonderful relationship, but only they knew the struggles of adjusting, especially with the clear evidence of the previous marriage always there in the form of my presence. It could not have been easy for them.

Eight years without a father and then a new stepfather certainly impacted me with both wounds and strengths. The bonds of father and son never developed in a classic way with my stepfather. There were many struggles and conflicts as I exerted my independence. Some of the normal fatherly discipline was absent. I never remember being disciplined by my stepfather. Perhaps he never felt he had the right. Would I have been more secure with my natural father? Would I have had a different childhood? Certainly, but I cannot say it would have been better or more healthy. The loss was history and I had to make the best of it.

The Opposite of Loss

The opposite of a loss is a win. From our earliest days, we are taught the joy, and importance, of winning. Boys are inculcated with the idea that it is imperative to win—in sports, arguments, war, board games, and life in general. We applaud when our children win a game, make a shot, get a hit, score a goal, or star in a drama at school. We comfort them when they fail. We watch their emotions soar and sink. The not-so-subtle message is that it is good to win and bad to lose. We try to teach them to be good sports (that is, good losers), and we believe that deeply. But we also communicate that it is better to win.

> *The not-so-subtle message is that it is good to win and bad to lose. We try to teach them to be good sports (that is, good losers), and we believe that deeply. But we also communicate that it is better to win.*

I play games with my grandchildren. In most games I can easily win (though that is not the case with the new reflexive computer games). If they win, they are elated. They laugh and clap. They love to beat me. If I win, they are sober and ask for another game. Right there, they are learning to cope with loss and compare the joys and sorrows of winning and losing. But inside there still resides the deep desire to win.

We want them to be winners. We want to build their self-esteem. We want them to be confident. We also want them to know how to handle defeat, since everyone cannot be a winner. In life every man will face critical issues of loss which will either build his character or destroy his will to keep growing as a man.

We face many losses in life: death, job, disappointment, money, and relationships. Several primary losses affect men deeply, sneaking up on them, and subtly endangering their well-being. These include loss of motivation, loss of position, loss of influence, loss of identity, and loss of confidence. These losses strike most deeply at a man's ego and being. To a great extent they are inevitable. It is just a matter of time until one or more of these losses challenge *your* life—and place *you* in danger. They are what I call *the predictable losses of life.* Though I call them *predictable* they nevertheless usually surprise us, catching us unprepared. Over the next five chapters, we'll look at these predictable losses in more depth.

QUESTIONS FOR THOUGHT AND DISCUSSION

1. What losses have affected your life? How did you respond to them?

2. Were these losses expected or completely out of the blue?

3. Why is the manner in which we face or deal with our losses so vital to the development of our character?

SCRIPTURAL INSIGHTS:

1. Compare Saul and Joseph (1 Samuel 15:10-35 and Genesis 39). What were their losses? What was the difference in their responses?

CHAPTER THREE

LOSS OF MOTIVATION

SOCIOLOGISTS and business researchers have tried for decades to define motivation. They have studied human behavior and tried to learn how to motivate people. Psychologists and psychiatrists deal daily with people who have lost their motivation and become seriously depressed. Hundreds of books have been written to help a person move toward self-motivation. The solutions they recommend range from manipulative self-actualization, to accumulation of wealth, to recounting personal success experiences, to just plain "hype" designed to sell a book.

Motivational seminars abound — in person, on cassette, on videotapes. We all feel a deep need to be motivated and motivational.

There are no easy answers since motivation is one of the most intangible of qualities. We are men with individual personalities, needs, backgrounds, experiences, and intellects. No one formula will work. Sometimes we despair that anything will work.

It Affects Every Man

One thing is sure. At some point, every man will suffer moderate to severe loss of motivation. When it happens we become confused. We recognize it, but feel powerless to change our feelings.

It is frightening, especially for men who are used to being motivated and excited about life.

It is frightening, especially for men who are used to being motivated and excited about life. There comes a sense of purposelessness, a lack of drive, a feeling that nothing matters. An inability to act takes over. Critical tasks remain undone. Going to work is drudgery. And all of this spills over into family life, causing conflicts and misunderstandings.

Causes of Motivational Loss

What causes this precipitous decrease in motivation? Many things may trigger it: loss of a job, perceived or real failure, marriage problems, illness, fatigue, stress, age, or boredom.

I have experienced various swings in motivation over the years. In 1990 a severe loss threw me into a lingering period when my motivation stayed at a low ebb. In April of 1990 my 30-year-old son was brutally murdered while working at one of his two jobs. He broadcast his own show on local public radio and drove his own taxi to put bread on the table. One night a customer simply set out to kill someone. And that someone who answered the call for a taxi was my son.

Shock and grief overwhelmed our lives for months. Prior to this tragic event, much of my motivational being was consumed by leading The Navigators and helping people grow spiritually. It was a tremendous challenge and still is! But after Steve's death, it seemed that nothing mattered anymore. It put every activity of my life in a different perspective. My life went on "hold." Even spiritual activities seemed trivial and inconsequential. I wondered if purpose and motivation would ever return. Weeks and months went by as I continued in my leadership task, knowing that I was not "all there." People were very patient and understanding. My motivation grew back slowly as I recovered from grief.

Motivation returned but in a very different form. Position and responsibility mattered little. A purifying and cleansing had taken place in my soul. I viewed life—and death—differently. I spent much time wrestling with some critical biblical issues: God's sovereignty, God's goodness, prayer . . . all those puzzling "whys" of life. My wife Mary has written extensively about this time of our lives in her book *Harsh Grief, Gentle Hope*.[1]

Even the apostle Paul experienced this loss of motivation, referring to himself as "depressed." In 2 Corinthians 7:6, in the midst of conflict and fear, he says: "For even when we came into Macedonia our flesh had no rest, but we were afflicted on every side: conflicts without, fears within" (2 Corinthians 7:5, NASB).

Deeper Issues

I can relate to that. Conflicts, problems, and pressures are all around. Fears and turmoil capture my mind and soul. And in the midst of the havoc, motivation disappears. Trying to identify the reasons may help, but the conflicts and fears remain just the same.

Many paths lead to a loss of motivation. Personality is a factor. So is age and stage of life. Life traumas contribute. Failing health exacerbates the problem. Sometimes we call it burnout.

We despise the feelings and silently cry to be rescued.

But that is the problem. The cry is usually silent. Men find it so difficult to call for help. We go on and suffer in silence rather than admit the weakness we have seen in ourselves. "After all, what will people think? I'll lose respect. I may lose my job. I'll just gut it out. It'll go away."

Sometimes it does go away. But then deeper issues of our lives still rumble inwardly, unheard and unmet. Some of these issues stem from our more evil side—the love of money, the love of power, the desire for comfort and material accumulation, the exercise of authority, or the domination of people. Other issues arise out of our insecurities. Am I liked? Do people respect me? What if I don't achieve my potential? What if I fail?

Biblical Solutions and Basic Motivations

This topic of motivation has been studied extensively in this century, especially as it relates to workers and productivity. Much has been written on self-motivation and managerial motivation. For the last twelve years I have studied motivation to discover biblical solutions. I found that most secular motivational techniques were manipulative and coercive. The Christian counterparts were largely warmed-over secular ideas with some spiritual vocabulary and a few verses. Even today, I am not prepared to write a full book on the subject. I know there are deep roots of motivation which go beyond the surface psychological indicators we all experience.

> *As long as the desire remains strong, we remain motivated. When the desire wanes, our motivation disappears. And it will wane. Desire is not ultimately the best foundation for motivation.*

Basic motivations find roots in desire (lust), fear, and love. We are motivated to do some things out of great *desire* to make money, achieve education, be promoted, get married, maintain a good marriage. As long as the desire remains strong, we remain motivated. When the desire wanes, our motivation disappears. And it will wane. Desire is not ultimately the best foundation for motivation.

Fear is an incredibly effective motivation. It is a basic instrument of survival. Fear of losing a job, losing respect, losing a marriage, or failing often keeps us going. But fear as a basic motivation is short lived. It only works for a brief time before it eats at our inner person and erupts in anger and rebellion.

The Greatest Motivator

The greatest of all motivations is *love*. It is the least used or under-stood in our modern world. In spite of considerable teaching on relationships, people skills, values, and equality, we still do not grasp the simple power of love. Love of God. Love of people. Love of ourselves. Each of these loves brings a dimension to motivation that makes desire and fear look weak. But it is too simple an answer, too easily said. We need to know *how* to develop love as a basis for our motivation.

Desire and fear are counterfeits of love. Desire becomes lust, just as sexual love easily becomes lust. Fear is the replacement of love. "There is no fear in love; but perfect love casts out fear, because fear involves punishment" (1 John 4:18, NASB). We inflict fear or respond to fear when love is missing. Love is a difficult emotion for a man, yet it is the key to motivation. More on this later in a larger context.

Natural Motivators

Before leaving this discussion let us ask, "Are desire and fear illegit-imate motivators?" Not entirely. Desire is a natural human drive — for food and nourishment, for love and security, for pleasure and comfort. When desire has a root in God and His Word, it becomes holy. Desire relates to the longings of our heart. These longings are placed within us by God. Men often find it difficult to express the deepest longings of the heart. These are longings for things only God can fully supply — longings to be holy, to do good, to be a man of integrity, to be

> *Fear is also a legitimate motivator as long as it is properly focused.*

respected, and to be used by God. We have tasted these longings, but most often it has been just a taste. We need a feast. Then we will experience real motivation from desire.

Fear is also a legitimate motivator as long as it is properly focused. "Fear God, and keep His commandments" (Ecclesiastes 12:13). "The fear of the Lord is the beginning of wisdom" (Proverbs 9:10).

God is to be feared for He alone has the true power of judgment. We can be secure in His love, as a child is secure in a father's love. A child has a healthy fear of the father that leads to obedience and doing what is right. We need that motivation. But it is legitimate only in relation to God, not men.

Overcoming Motivational Fears

Major Jack Wyman was a hard-working, dedicated Air Force officer. After leaving one of the best assignments in the Air Force, he was assigned to a job outside the country. He performed superbly. The officer who wrote his performance review was in the United States and did not really know Jack personally. "Out of sight, out of mind" governed his rating. He did not give Jack the top rating. Although this was disappointing, it was not the end of the world.

The promotion board met to select people for lieutenant colonel. When the list came out, he did not receive a call of congratulations from his commander. The silence was deafening.

The next day the list was published. He was not on it. He had been passed over. He knew his career was destroyed. He didn't want to talk to anyone. He was embarrassed and crushed. His motivation for work flew out the window. Getting up to go to work was a chore. It seemed that he no longer could.

Then he began to think—and pray. Was not God sovereign? Was this the worst thing that could happen to him? He began to see his entire career in a different light. He determined to continue to work hard and to keep going. He found himself thanking God for the trial.

When he went on mandatory retirement as a major, he saw it as a great opportunity. He not only survived, but regained his motivation, launching into a successful second career. He had lost his fear of failure. Inevitably our motivation will wane or even disappear for a period of time. The danger is not losing motivation as much as how we respond to that loss. If God is the source of our life, then He will sustain us through this dampening of our human motivation.

As you read this book let me encourage you to follow the leading of the Holy Spirit in the areas He has pointed out to you. It is a matter of life and death—of spiritual survival.

As Larry Crabb puts it: "Nothing matters more than developing a passion for Christ as we try to handle life's struggles responsibly and wisely. Our primary purpose is not to use God to solve problems but to move through our problems toward finding God."[2]

That is our overriding purpose—to know Christ more deeply and to follow Him with all our heart. Remember the words of missionary martyr Jim Elliot, "He is no fool who gives what he cannot keep, to gain that which he cannot lose."

Now we turn to the next loss that is often the source of a man's motivation—position.

QUESTIONS FOR THOUGHT AND DISCUSSION

1. Have you gone through periods of loss of motivation? What brought you through? In retrospect, can you see root causes for that loss of motivation?

2. Why are our desires, even good desires, insufficient to keep us motivated for a lifetime?

3. What problems are caused when fear is the primary motivating principle in a man's life?

4. Can fear and desire be legitimate motivating factors? When?

5. What causes you to lose motivation? Do you face it alone or do you have other people you trust with whom you can discuss the issue?

6. If you have not experienced a loss of motivation, how can you prepare now to deal with such a time when it comes?

7. How are purpose and motivation related?

SCRIPTURAL INSIGHTS:

1. What motivated Paul in Philippians 1:12-26?

CHAPTER FOUR

LOSS OF POSITION

Every man eventually loses his position. It may be at retirement. But eventually it disappears. Position describes the roles we hold in life — manager, foreman, designer, engineer, salesman, farmer, owner, supervisor, machine operator, deacon, elder, father, and husband. All are temporary. With the exception of family roles, position seldom lasts for a lifetime.

I have talked with men who have lost their jobs. Pain fills their eyes. Their voices are dull. Nothing strikes at the ego of a man like being out of work. It reveals our great dependence on what we do for our identity. No matter how much we may believe we are above that kind of identification, we still inwardly depend on it. Our value, our drive, our personhood inextricably become intertwined with our work. Even the man who hates his job still receives much of his identity from it. "What do you do?" becomes a feared question when one no longer has a job or position.

One of my friends was removed from his managerial responsibilities. Later he lost his job. He expressed and shared his pain. He admitted it—and also hated his feelings and responses. He could not shake them off by simply admitting them. Inner feelings are not always controlled by the mind or reason. Loss of position is like a small death.

Loss of position is like a small death.

When position dies, many areas of our lives are affected. We become more focused on money. Our marriages begin to show strain. Little conflicts with our wives become big conflicts. Our children begin to see a change in us as we turn our attention from them to ourselves. Even our friendships and our health suffer if we take this loss of position too seriously. But how else can a man take it?

One of the motivating factors in our work is to solidify our position. We work diligently to gain greater position. Isn't that career progression? Fear of losing position drives many men to a cut-throat view of life at work. This is a dead-end road. At some point we will lose. One businessman told me that at the end of each day he would call a friend and ask, "Did you draw any blood today?" Work was a form of war. Winning meant spilling blood. Losing position was not an option.

Although this loss of position often occurs in the workplace, it also occurs in many other areas of life. Divorce robs us of the position of husband and father. The egos of both men and women are severely damaged by the failure of a marriage. The loss devastates multiple victims. The loss of position at work fades in significance to the loss of divorce. But then work takes on a new challenge to prove ourselves and counter the loss in the home.

Loss also comes about when our job is eliminated or disappears through change, downsizing, or lack of performance. This is the ultimate loss of position in the work world.

Even in the church we become position dependent. Elders,

deacons, teachers, and committee members are all positions of responsibility which give a certain status in a congregation. Conflict, growth of the church, and growing older all can precipitate a loss of position. Many men who have little recognition or position in the working world often turn to position in the church. This is not wrong—just a fact. In that context a great contribution can be made.

What is the big deal about position? Why is it such an important thing to men? From our earliest days as children we are taught by parents, school, role models, and the media that titles and position reflect success and accomplishment. Authority, respect, and honor are given to people of certain positions. It is a fact of society. As early as the elementary school years elections and selections take place— class president, secretary, student of the week. These are excellent means of building self-esteem and confidence. I applaud them. But like so many good things they communicate other messages that linger in our minds for a lifetime. I am not at all in favor of a class-less society or of making no distinctions for ability and responsibility. But when one becomes an adult, new thinking needs to emerge. Achievement is important. Success is important. Let's not downgrade it, but rather let's live with the inevitable fact that it is temporary—and not the source of our identity or worth.

For several years in The Navigators we have been taught that in God's economy position is less important than function. We have tried to downplay titles and a hierarchical view of leadership and to emphasize teamwork and task. Yet human nature being what it is, people and organizations still invent or attach a scaled meaning to certain jobs. Man is insatiably position oriented—especially in the Western world. In other parts of the world different criteria are used for "positioning"—age, heritage, or education, for instance.

So let's accept two realities. First, position is a fact of life—a necessary and useful fact of life. Second, every position is ultimately temporary and will disappear.

Maxing Out

In addition to losing position, there is the reality of "maxing out"— reaching the limit of our abilities or opportunities and being denied the next promotion. In the military, reaching the rank of full colonel is an honor achieved by only about 5 percent of all officers. One friend was not only a colonel, but was selected to serve in a brigadier general position and compete for that rank. However, he was not promoted. He suffered a blow to his ego. He nearly refused to have a retirement ceremony as a colonel. Yet if he had not had the opportunity for the next rank, he would have been thrilled to retire as a colonel.

The Bible records many stories of men who lost their positions. The key insight into their character is in each man's reaction to his respective losses.

That will happen to all of us. At some point younger people or others more qualified will take our place and we will step aside. Loss of position is inevitable.

The Bible records many stories of men who lost their positions. The key insight into their character is in each man's reaction to his respective losses.

When God rejected Saul, Israel's first king, Saul fought tooth and nail to keep his position. He murdered, schemed, and blasphemed God in the process. Eventually he committed suicide by falling on his sword.

David, his successor, later accepted God's punishment when he violated his position and was chased out of his palace. He submitted to God's sovereign decision.

Consequences of Positional Loss

Significant consequences result from loss of position. Finances can be greatly reduced. Embarrassment certainly accompanies the loss. Public status changes significantly. People view a man differently. Anger, bitterness, and loss of self-esteem create inner turmoil. These reactions provide fertile ground for God to work deeply in our character. Loss offers an opportunity to test character. Though painful, loss presents one of the greatest growth opportunities of life.

Handling Positional Loss

Mike had given his life to his company. He succeeded in almost everything he did. He was rewarded by promotion after promotion. Finally he became president and chief executive officer of the company. He had reached the pinnacle of his career. His first two years were rocky, but successful. Then he made a series of bold, strategic moves which damaged the company financially. After several months of trying to pull the company through the difficulties, he was asked to resign. It was as though his entire life was being torn apart. Embarrassment and a sense of failure engulfed him.

He decided that this was God at work in his life. He graciously stepped aside, helping his successor get started. He was offered the leadership of a major division of the company. Quite a step down. Rather than allowing himself to become bitter or discouraged, he took the new position with energy and gusto. His respect grew significantly within the company and others observed him overcome adversity and serve the company rather than himself.

What are the facts of position?

- Position is good and necessary in life and society.
- We place value on position.
- Every position is temporary.
- Loss of position is inevitable. Only the timing is in question.

When we understand and bring these facts into perspective, we can more easily surrender our position, realizing it does not define who we are. As we see position from God's viewpoint we become free, allowing Him to use it, change it, or eliminate it. Psalm 75:6,7 (KJV) has helped me. "For promotion cometh neither from the east, nor from the west, nor from the south. But God is the judge: He putteth down one, and setteth up another."

Even when a man does not have a position, there is something even more significant—his personal influence. What happens, then, when we lose this influence?

QUESTIONS FOR THOUGHT AND DISCUSSION

1. Why is loss of position inevitable?

2. Why is so much of our value and identity as men derived from work?

3. Does viewing positions as temporary affect your thinking about your current position? If so, how?

4. What are some responses to losing one's position?

5. How can you help younger men, who may still be ascending in whatever structure they are in, keep position in perspective?

6. How does our culture influence our view of position?

7. What are some identifiable seasons when loss of position is likely and can be thought about ahead of time?

SCRIPTURAL INSIGHTS:

1. Consider again Saul in 1 Samuel 15–18. What was the crucial turning point in his life? How could Saul have recovered from his initial mistake?

CHAPTER FIVE

LOSS OF INFLUENCE

HE sat in the gate to the city. An unusually handsome man, he was the son of the king. People were naturally drawn to him. He was the consummate politician, intercepting the people coming to plead their case for justice before the king. He lied, telling them they would not receive a hearing for their case, but, of course, he would gladly hear them if he were in a position of power. "So Absalom stole away the hearts of the men of Israel" (2 Samuel 15:6, NASB). He was a traitor to his father, King David, and soon staged a coup.

David fled Jerusalem for his life as his son attacked the city. Ahithophel, who had been a trusted counselor to David, joined the conspiracy. Ahithophel took on the role of chief counselor to Absalom in the new power structure. He seemed invincible in his counsel. "And the advice of Ahithophel, which he gave in those days, was as if one inquired of the word of God; so was all the advice of Ahithophel regarded by both David and Absalom" (2 Samuel 16:23, NASB). Talk about influence! He had it! He was riding the crest of his career.

Then something disastrous happened. David's advisor, Hushai, spoke to Absalom, convincing him to go against Ahithophel's counsel. What was Ahithophel's response? "Now when Ahithophel saw that his counsel was not followed, he saddled his donkey and arose and went to his home, to his city, and set his house in order, and strangled himself" (2 Samuel 17:23, NASB).

> *He seemed invincible in his counsel. Talk about influence! He had it! He was riding the crest of his career.*

All because he lost his influence. A sad end to a stellar career. His first mistake came when he sided with Absalom. He demonstrated great error of judgment. His doom was sealed. He tragically compounded his error by reacting to his loss of influence in the king's court. He took the ultimate step of rejection—suicide.

Not everyone can have a position of power or responsibility in our society like Ahithophel. But everyone does have influence. Each of us relishes making a difference or being influential in others' lives or in some small part of society.

The Nature of Influence

We influence our children and grandchildren. We influence friends, coworkers, and other believers. In all likelihood we are an expert in some skill or field. So people ask our help and counsel.

But that, too, will one day be lost. It may diminish slowly or be catastrophically destroyed.

Influence Comes In Many Forms

Influence is pervasive and multifaceted. There is the influence of your *person*—who you are. Your personality, character, experience, age, and wisdom all make up who you are. You may never have held a great position, but people still come to you for advice or counsel. You could be a youth leader, an elder, or just a good listener.

Varieties of Influence

I know people in The Navigators who are not in the leadership structure because that is not their gift. But they are godly and wise. They have great insight and godly counsel. They have depth of character. They wield incredible influence. They are sought out for their *godly wisdom and counsel*. This is their gift.

> *God sovereignly puts people in positions of power to be His instruments for good in a society. Such was the case with William Wilberforce, who was instrumental in the fight against slavery in England of the 1800s.*

Then there is influence of *performance*. Some people are incredibly skilled and gifted in leadership: speaking, managing, organizing, strategy, thinking, projects, manual skills, getting things done, selling, analyzing, or in technical or mechanical skills. Their performance and track records open doors of influence. We regularly see top management in successful corporations get drawn to another company. They are sought after. In every field of work, performance earns you the right to be heard. Often their abilities lead them to *positions* of influence.

Through the years I have met a number of top military leaders. They are gifted in leading and thinking. Unlike politics, they did not get to the top primarily by money or persuasion. They attained their positions by their skilled performance.

Others have an influence of *knowledge*. Usually through education and personal intellectual ability, they develop a reservoir of information, specialized knowledge, or analytical tools which pave the way for their influence. In politics and business they become special counselors and advisors. In the church body we see theologians and thinkers who influence by their knowledge.

Some wield influence by *power and wealth*. This can be used for good or evil purposes. God sovereignly puts people in positions of power to be His instruments for good in a society. Such was the case with William Wilberforce, who was instrumental in the fight against slavery in England of the 1800s. Today there are many political, government, and industry officials who use their influence for God. On the other hand, some use their power for selfish ends or even for evil goals.

The Influence of Wealth

Wealth is a relative term. Any amount of money above what is needed to live comfortably can be considered wealth. Some analysts of our world believe wealth is the driving force behind all world power. Certainly it is a major driving force. When an individual possesses even moderate wealth it exerts a profound effect on the way he thinks and acts. It gives the illusion of influence of *person* though it is actually the influence of *money*. Nothing is more fleeting. When one realizes the nature of the influence, it can be used for great good—the funding of many benevolent and missionary activities in this needy world. It can also be used for evil.

People who have some measure of wealth must realize that their personhood is not in their wealth. "For the love of money is the first step toward all kinds of sin. Some people have even turned away from God because of their love for it, and as a result have pierced themselves with many sorrows" (1 Timothy 6:10, TLB). It is so easy to lose sight of that vital fact.

Whether influence comes from person, performance, knowledge, power, or wealth, one thing is certain—it *will* fade. So often the reason for lessened influence is our own doing.

The Most Valuable Influence

The influence of person is the most valuable of all forms of influence. It is also extremely vulnerable. "As dead flies give perfume a bad smell, so a little folly outweighs wisdom and honor" (Ecclesiastes

10:1). "A good name is more desirable than great riches; to be esteemed is better than silver or gold" (Proverbs 22:1).

No one can remove your influence of person. Only you can. A little sin can ruin the greatest of reputations. The news around the Christian community attests to that fact. Except in rare cases, sin destroys influence and reputation for years, if not for a lifetime. Recovery of that influence, though not impossible, is exceedingly difficult.

> *Except in rare cases, sin destroys influence and reputation for years, if not for a lifetime.*

Our performance must eventually fade as age and diminished capacity reduce our effectiveness. Like an aging athlete, some of our top performances will be memories of the past. In the secular world, the pattern is to cast off even the best of past performances. What matters in the world is "what can you do for me now?" If you have experienced this loss you know the feelings of betrayal that come with these events.

Two Great Examples

As I think about influence, I cannot help but think of J. Oswald Sanders, a friend and mentor of mine. Oswald was nearing his ninetieth birthday when he died—working on his last book (several books were his "last book"). At age fifty he left a prosperous career as an attorney in New Zealand to lead the China Inland Mission (now Overseas Missionary Fellowship)—quite a step down from that esteemed position in his secular society.

After several years of leading the mission, he retired, only to take on the directorship of a Christian college. Another step downward in the eyes of even the Christian world. Then he retired again. After being a widower twice, he certainly deserved a rest. But rather than lying back and taking it easy, he accelerated, spending his last twenty years speaking around the world over 300 times per year. His influence grew rather than diminished. His respect grew even though he never sought the limelight or tried to maintain his position.

Though Oswald never complained, I'm certain each of his

changes in life came with some trauma and loss. Certainly his personal losses were great. What was perceived as a loss of influence became the stair steps to greater influence.

Certainly one man who seemed to lose everything in terms of position, authority, and influence was Chuck Colson. As a man ensconced in power alongside former president Nixon, Chuck Colson pulsated with power and influence. And he used them with skill and mastery.

Then in the midst of the Watergate scandal, his world collapsed. When the storm subsided, he found himself in prison with no hope or future. He was washed up. Finished. Down for the count.

In *Born Again* he tells the story of his fall, his finally understanding that his only hope was in Jesus Christ, and his personal conversion. He was a man with no influence, but now he had personal hope. As he began to put the pieces of his life back together, he quietly developed a personal burden for prisoners and their families. Out of this burden the Prison Fellowship ministry developed; then came Justice Fellowship (a ministry to the judiciary), and finally Neighbors Who Care (a ministry to victims of crime).

Today Chuck Colson has influence all over the nation as a respected and listened-to statesman. His shattered influence grew back to an influence of greater and lasting magnitude.

Your Own Influence

You may be saying, I'm no J. Oswald Sanders or Chuck Colson. No, but you can be—perhaps not in such a public way. I have known many men who lost their obvious position and influence (power) but who kept going. They grew in character and depth. Some had begun to use their influence in different ways. They traded influence of power for influence of person. They adjusted their lives to this new circumstance, seeing the hand of God in their history and future.

Knowledge is the most constant of these areas of influence. Yet, as time goes on, fewer and fewer young people will seek our counsel and knowledge.

One older Navigator staff person told me sadly, "I know all the answers, but no one asks me questions anymore."

There is also the distinct possibility that our knowledge becomes outdated. To keep influencing others, we must keep current. Knowledge of the Word never fades, but must remain fresh and relevant. The quickest way for influence to be lost, short of sin, is to have an ax to grind or a prejudiced stand on issues. Younger people do not want to know how we did it in the old days. If we insist on presenting ancient history they will be polite, listen, but not inquire again.

Power and wealth are as fleeting as a puff of smoke. As soon as they wane, the influence disappears. I have seen a number of people in the last two decades undergo financial setbacks or bankruptcy, hard times, and lawsuits. In many cases they experienced a loss of friends, a loss of respect, and sensed a general distancing from the Christian community that once courted their favor.

Influence, properly used, is a gift from God. It is largely temporary and especially vulnerable. Guard it by being enamored with your God, not your influence.

QUESTIONS FOR THOUGHT AND DISCUSSION

1. What factors contribute to one's ability to influence another?

2. In which areas of your life do you wield influence?

3. What are some of the ways that we undermine our ability to influence others?

4. How can you handle the influences of wealth or power without becoming dependent on them?

5. How can you prepare for periods or seasons of life when loss of influence is likely?

SCRIPTURAL INSIGHTS:

1. From Hebrews 13:7 what should be our greatest influence? How do verses 1-6 shed light on the meaning of verse 7?

CHAPTER SIX

LOSS OF IDENTITY

And when they died,
it was as though they had never lived.

FROM *OF HUMAN BONDAGE*

Is that reality? Once people have passed from their "useful" times of life, are they no longer valid? Do they just fade into the past like a dim memory, sitting in a nursing home, visited by tolerant relatives who would rather be somewhere else? Everything inside us cries out, "No!" for we know that one day that will be our destiny. I have seen many men leave various positions of responsibility. Two left a lasting impression on me because of their contrast.

A close friend served under a dynamic four star general in the army. The retirement parade was everything you would expect for a departing hero. Parties and special dinners filled the weeks before his retirement. He left in a blaze of glory.

About two years later the general lay in a hospital. He was dying. My friend, a chaplain, visited him. He rather innocently asked, "What was it like leaving such great responsibility and becoming an ordinary citizen?" Bitterness filled the general's voice as he replied, "We drove off the base in our recreational vehicle. Now I commanded nothing except the steering wheel on my RV—and my wife told me where to turn that!"

He died without purpose, having lost the only identity he valued.

In sharp contrast was Lieutenant General William K. Harrison. I remember talking to him about his career. He never achieved what he desired—a major fighting command. He was selected by General Douglas MacArthur to be the first chief negotiator after the Korean War. He became known as "the Christian General." He was highly respected at all levels.

> *He became known as "the Christian General." He was highly respected at all levels.*

When General Harrison retired, he stepped out into a new life with the vigor and optimism of a young man. His identity and self-image were not in being a general. He went on to serve on a seminary board, wrote a book on eschatology, and was in demand as a speaker.

Each of these men reached the end of his life having had a similar human identity, but a radically different view of his real identity.

We know the day is coming when we will be feeble and old. Who knows what we will cling to as an identity at that time? What happens when we lose our identity in the prime of life? That loss affects each of us in a much different way.

Establishing Your Identity

Have you ever been in a social situation where no one knows you? Where no one pays any attention to you? You meet people, and they give you a nod and move on. Your mind starts scheming for some way of establishing your identity. Usually, a first move is to let them know what your work is. "I'm an engineer. I'm an attorney. I'm a builder. I'm a machinist. I'm an electrician. I'm a teacher." All of these occupations provide us with a temporary identity. Then we begin to spell out which layer of the hierarchy we occupy. Project engineer, vice president, partner, foreman, etc. Now we feel our identity is more solid.

Other nuances of our identity struggle to emerge and give more substance to our ego identity—our wealth, who we know, our accomplishments, the size of our home, our hobbies. Unconsciously, we build up an identity to which we cling all too tightly. I am not guiltless in this game. Many times I have found myself letting people know "who I really am." Sometimes it is for a legitimate connection with others, but all too often it is for my own ego identity.

Does this sound like a familiar pattern? Regardless of the strata of society in which we live, each label has peculiar value, like hunting, fishing, golf, money, boats, or clothes. Through the years we build and protect this identity.

Losing Your Identity

What happens when you lose that identity? And you will. You will retire, be demoted, fired, move, or lose that identity in some way. Then the impact of the phrase, "I am what I do," begins to sink in. That's not who you really are, of course. But it is, in reality, how we think and feel. For men, identity is so wrapped up in our work that we do not, or cannot, envision ourselves apart from it. This is why unemployment is so devastating to a man's ego. That is why so many men die within two years of retirement.

When we lose our work identity, we are faced with the question, "Who am I?" It is an appropriate question—one we should have faced years ago.

This concept of identity, intertwining with work, is a two-edged sword. For those in higher positions, losing it is traumatic. For many who spend their lives (as did my stepfather) in more mundane jobs, they face the unspoken response, "Oh, you're just a _____." Fill in the blank with truck driver, factory worker, janitor, day laborer, store clerk, or any job that does not pay well or does not require recognized, special skills.

How many mothers boast, "My son digs ditches"? They want to say, "He's a doctor. He's a corporate officer." Many men cringe at their identity in the lower rungs of employment, wishing that people would give them credit for their intelligence, integrity, or family life. Minorities in our society feel this all too strongly, being placed in certain boxes of society. They are frequently judged by their skin color or ethnic origins, not their abilities.

Moving Beyond a Wrong View of Identity

As a person of reasonable spiritual maturity, I thought I had moved beyond this wrong view of my personhood. I come from a simple, lower-income family. I was the first in my family to attend a university. I found much of my new identity related to my education and being an Air Force officer.

> *How many mothers boast, "My son digs ditches"? They want to say, "He's a doctor. He's a corporate officer."*

Recently, I remarked to Mary, "You know, there are some titles that stay with you for a lifetime — and I have two of them: doctor and general." I began the statement as a praise to God, but even in saying that I revealed my own focus on identity. I was as afflicted with the problem as any other man. And I don't like the thought that I have not progressed any further.

It is hard to describe to people what The Navigators do, and it is especially difficult to describe to nonbelievers. When I am asked what I do, I often reply by telling what I used to do — I served on the faculty of the U.S. Air Force Academy or I worked in the space program. The identity struggle is always present. Some of the struggle relates to pride. Some of it resides in our humanity.

In the Bible, people are referred to as Elijah the prophet, David the king, Paul the apostle, Peter the fisherman, or Matthew the tax collector.

All of us will eventually lose our work-related identities. We will become a "used to be." The shock will come when we realize how much that identity meant to us. We will feel a deep sense of loss.

Many men will suffer depression. Many will die early in the void of their identity. The more our personhood is wrapped up in our external identity, the more the loss will impact us.

The True Source of Identity

God clearly teaches the real source of identity in the Bible. Our identity is in Christ. We are sons and daughters of God, believers in Christ. God also gave us valid identities which distinguish us for a lifetime—human being, friend, neighbor, servant, father, husband. These identities can be wounded or broken, but they are legitimate and fulfilling identities upon which we can build.

Paul was a man of great accomplishments, but counted them worthless compared to his identity in Christ. He reflected some of these thoughts in Philippians 3:4-9:

> Though I myself have reasons for such confidence. If anyone else thinks he has reasons to put confidence in the flesh, I have more: circumcised on the eighth day, of the people of Israel, of the tribe of Benjamin, a Hebrew of Hebrews; in regard to the law, a Pharisee; as for zeal, persecuting the church; as for legalistic righteousness, faultless. But whatever was to my profit I now consider loss for the sake of Christ. What is more, I consider everything a loss compared to the surpassing greatness of knowing Christ Jesus my Lord, for whose sake I have lost all things. I consider them rubbish, that I may gain Christ and be found in him, not having a righteousness of my own that comes from the law, but that which is through faith in Christ—the righteousness that comes from God and is by faith.

This is a good theory, good teaching, but difficult to apply if it has not been a part of our foundation *before* the loss comes.

When my son was murdered, it was the spiritual roots that had grown deep earlier in my life that allowed me to draw upon the strength and comfort of God. My theology was tested, but my belief in the goodness and sovereignty of God deepened. Even more significant was the change in my identity as a man. Suddenly work and accomplishments meant almost nothing. Those things which previously fed my ego disappeared. My identity as a father, husband, friend, and frail human being emerged and deepened. My identity as a child of God took on new meaning, as did life itself.

Shifting from our identity based on human accomplishments to one based on our place as a child of God is a lifelong process. Any other identity will fail. Let's begin growing an identity that will last a lifetime.

QUESTIONS FOR THOUGHT AND DISCUSSION

1. How do we disentangle our identity from work?

2. What happens when we build our identity on something temporary?

3. Why is having your identity in Christ so important? What does this mean?

4. What are some of the more permanent aspects of our identities as fathers, husbands, friends, etc.?

SCRIPTURAL INSIGHTS:

1. The phrases "in Him" and "in Christ" are used several times in Ephesians 1:1-14. What does this mean? Consider Ephesians 4:17-24. How does finding our identity in Christ unshackle us from tying our identity too closely to work, other persons, our possessions?

2. What was Paul's attitude toward worldly possessions and accomplishments? (Philippians 2)

CHAPTER SEVEN

LOSS OF CONFIDENCE

PERSONAL confidence is a mystery. Some people have it. Some don't. Confidence is self-reliance, the positive feeling that we can conquer the problems of life. We want our children to develop confidence — to learn to walk, hit a baseball, recite a poem, build models, catch a football, play an instrument, or give a speech.

We remember the encouragement we gave to our babies to take their first steps. We watched them abruptly sit down rather than try taking steps. We may remember our own fear or loss of confidence when we tried out for a ball team or embarked on some new experience.

When our children go to school we want them to be confident

and develop a healthy self-esteem. I remember each of my children going through times of shyness, fear, and timidity. We work with their fragile egos to encourage them, cheering at the smallest success, comforting them in each small failure.

I clearly recall a confidence-building incident in my senior year of high school. In the years that followed my separation from my grandfather, I lost my confidence. I became a believer in Christ before entering high school. My first semester as a high school freshman I performed in an average fashion. I received one A, two Bs, and two Cs.

Then I became a *committed* believer, making a definite commitment to the Lordship of Christ. A light turned on within me. I became a straight A student, graduating with honors. What a confidence booster! I realized I could accomplish, attain goals, and succeed.

Then an incident smashed my confidence.

I applied for a Navy ROTC scholarship at the University of Washington. I rode the Greyhound bus three hundred miles from Spokane to Seattle. I stayed overnight in the YMCA. The next morning I appeared before a Navy Captain for an interview. I was dressed in a sensible blue suit, a wash-and-wear ('50s style) white shirt with a wrinkled collar. I looked like a country bumpkin. I felt like one. I performed poorly in the interview.

When I said I liked music, the Captain began to quiz me about classical composers, where they were born, what they wrote, where they lived. I didn't have a clue. I had never studied classical music. I just liked to sing in the high school choir and play the accordion! I was embarrassed.

I was not awarded the scholarship. My confidence bubble burst. I went to the Air Force ROTC at the university as a default. Now as I serve as a Major General in the Air Force Reserves, the incident seems somewhat humorous. But it was humiliating at the time.

Self-Confidence: The Road to Success

As adult men we know that self-confidence paves the way to success in many ways. As we mature we learn our gifts and skills, develop them and use them with confidence. Some men possess great confidence and have the talent to back it up. Others succeed with less talent but with strong confidence — sometimes bordering on bravado. Others of us fear we will be found lacking, so we mask our inner insecurities by an outer confidence.

By age thirty most of us develop a reasonable confidence in ourselves and our work. Then if some confidence-shaking event invades our lives we feel we have been stripped bare. Whatever confidence we had begins to crumble.

I was embarrassed. I was not awarded the scholarship. My confidence bubble burst.

My twenties and thirties were generally filled with confidence-building events. In my Air Force and Navigator careers I experienced growing confidence and competence. At age forty the bottom fell out for me.

I had been directing two geographical regions for the Navigators. I worked hard, too hard. There were numerous personnel problems and conflicts that needed attention. Every trip was emotion-laden. Near the end of the first year of holding the two jobs I felt tired but realized the end was in sight, and I had some rest and recuperation time planned.

Suddenly, I was asked to move to another part of the country to take still another region. It was the straw that broke the camel's back for me. I reacted. I became angry. Then I was embarrassed at my public reaction. Depression set in. Everyone could see it, or so I thought. I was in physical and emotional burnout.

I recovered fairly quickly. But my confidence was gone. I felt I had no place speaking out in leadership meetings. I did not want any further responsibility. I felt I had failed. I imagined people talking about me: "Jerry has maxed out."

To that point my work in the Navigators had gone well. Now my pride and ego were wounded. My limitations had been tested and broken. I lost confidence.

Through this experience I learned many valuable lessons. Over time, my confidence returned but on a different, and hopefully better, foundation.

The Sources of Self-Confidence

Where does confidence come from?

Home Life

Personal and family background form many of the roots of confidence. Homes where children are affirmed and encouraged help build healthy self-confidence and self-esteem. Children who face constant criticism grow up thinking they are incapable and incompetent. At the opposite extreme, children who are relentlessly pushed to the limits of their ability for success and performance grow up thinking they can never please their parents, thus wounding their developing confidence.

No one has a perfect upbringing. But parents who are confident will encourage confidence in their children. So much is absorbed in the context of the family. Positive attitudes, affirmation, appropriate discipline, stable relationships, and love cultivate the soil of confidence. Neither affluence nor poverty determines confidence. We see people of confidence emerge from the most poverty-stricken homes as well as the wealthy environments. The key is what goes on inside the home.

Mary, my wife, comes from a very stable, godly family. She always knew she was loved even though discipline and legalism were high. I came from a divorced home, but still had love. Neither of our parents had much in the way of worldly wealth or position. Yet there was stability—each of our parents doing the best they knew to do in terms of encouragement. Could they have done better? Certainly. So could we with our children.

Regardless of your family background, you now have the responsibility to move forward in life. This is expressed by the writer Louis L' Amour:

> Up to a point a man's life is shaped by environment, heredity, and movements and changes in the world about him. Then there comes a time when it lies within his grasp to shape the clay of his life into the sort of thing he wishes to

be. Only the weak blame parents, their race, their times, lack of good fortune, or the quirks of fate. Everyone has it within his power to say *This I am today; that I will be tomorrow* (emphasis added).[1]

Whether Introvert or Extrovert

Personality plays a significant role in our confidence. It is not a matter of being an extrovert or an introvert. Some people just naturally exude confidence. External confidence does not always indicate internal confidence. Even a naturally confident person can be broken by the events of life.

Norm and I met about twenty-five years ago. He was a new believer in Christ, full of energy and optimism. He was extremely successful in sales with a major computer company. As I watched him through the years I observed him encounter many difficulties in life and business. Even when he was down, he was still positive and optimistic. This personality trait, combined with his growing faith, carried him through times when his confidence could have been destroyed. I often marveled at how he could be so positive. But that was simply the way God made him.

I think Norm did get discouraged. He wrestled internally with the "whys" of some of God's leading in his life. In fact, I suspect in some ways he was quite insecure, covering it with an external confidence.

One other friend, Andy, had a similar personality. He seemed always to be up even though I knew he had encountered some heavy issues in his life. But he was different from Norm. Andy never let it show. Norm did—at least to close friends. Later, Andy's life collapsed around him. He left his wife and family, destroying most of what had taken him a lifetime to build.

Natural Abilities and Performance

Competence is a tremendous confidence builder. Competence is simply the ability to perform a task well. Competence is a combination of natural gifts, training, and demonstrated experience. There are varying degrees of competence. Just as there are good teachers and great teachers, good football players and great football players, or good leaders and great leaders, so too are there varying degrees of competence.

We can always build competence in the areas in which we are gifted. Knowing our natural gifting is key to building competence. The apostle Paul instructs us to "think so as to have sound judgment" and "not to think more highly than we ought to think about ourselves."

Franklyn was a dropout from college. He didn't even finish the first part of the first semester! He simply got bored and quit. One of his goals in life was to make money—lots of it. He soon got involved in a very lucrative business which set him well on his way to financial success. In the process he discovered he was really good with figuring out investments and making profit.

He had called me one day and asked if I knew anyone in a prestigious national brokerage firm. I asked why. He said he wanted to pursue that as a career. Firms like the one he wanted to join were hiring only those with Harvard MBA's or the equivalent. I reminded him he had no qualifications or education to make them even want to look at him.

But he persisted, talking his way into being hired. He finished number one in their training program—at age 42! He went on to do spectacularly in the company. He was competent. It was clear that he had natural gifts at understanding finance and handling money.

It is amazing to see the transformation of confidence that occurs when a man is in a job that matches his gifts and enhances his competence. When Franklyn matched his gifts and his job, his confidence soared.

However, even when you are competent, there will always be those who are more competent. Competence itself will not protect your job or your ego. It is one factor. More is needed to put your confidence in the right place.

The Education Component

Education is a key component of confidence. Roland finished his stint in the Navy, having come to personal belief in Christ as a young sailor. He got his help from The Navigators, so he joined our training program at Glen Eyrie. It was a work/study/character building program, out of which some people came on our staff.

Roland had little education, came from a poor home, and was extremely awkward. He could hardly put together a grammatically complete sentence. Those who knew him thought he was mentally slow and soon ushered him on to other things. He returned to his home state and enrolled in college. There he (and others) found that he was far from slow — in fact he had a genius IQ.

In a society where such a high value is placed on technical or academic education we can never stop learning.

Education began to awaken his curiosity, intellect, and incredible ability to think. Today, he is a highly respected academician, author, and apologist of Christianity. He went from defeat and discouragement to fulfillment and accomplishment through both his dedication to God and education.

In a society where such a high value is placed on technical or academic education we can never stop learning. The pace of change in every area of our society requires us to keep pursuing education and development. For someone who has "stalled out" or has lost confidence, returning to further study may be the key to rebuilding.

In The Navigators I have seen many men whose lives were radically changed by their conversion experience. Even when they had no interest in schooling while in high school, now they hungered to learn. As with Franklyn, education then transformed their lives and confidence.

The School of Human Experience

Experience contributes significantly to build or destroy confidence. This is especially true in the human, secular realm. The cumulative experiences of life either build us up or break us down. We should never think that only successful experiences build confidence. Some of the most gifted and successful people in the world developed confidence through difficult and disastrous experiences. Through those experiences they developed both character and confidence.

Allen decided to go to a small Bible school rather than a university. People wondered what good that would do him since he did not plan to go into a full-time ministry position. He got a job with an airline, slowly working his way up in their marketing and management. Most of his contemporaries had education far beyond his.

> *Whatever the source, the root cause of the loss is a misplaced confidence. The only place we can safely put our confidence is in God.*

When Allen took an early retirement, it was just a matter of months before the company asked if he would come back to tackle a very difficult management task in another country. They wanted him specifically because of his experience, his character, and his demonstrated performance.

His past experience was not always easy, since he had determined to live by God's rules without compromise. He had not "cut corners" or succumbed to pressures to promote himself or act unethically. When the need arose for someone who was experienced and uncompromising in his standards, he was clearly the man.

Overcoming Confidence Shakers

Many events can shake our confidence. A few events can destroy it. Most confidence breakers relate to some failure or perceived failure in life and work. A poor performance review, loss of position, loss of job, a failed marriage, a public embarrassment, burnout, an emotional breakdown, an illness, or a bankruptcy can trigger this crisis of confidence deterioration. It can happen suddenly or over a long period of time. Repeated failures also lead to diminished confidence.

Whatever the source, the root cause of the loss is a misplaced confidence. The only place we can safely put our confidence is in God. The Bible talks about depending on either the flesh or the

Spirit. When the Bible speaks of the "flesh" it refers to our baser human drives—often the gratification of sin.

When we depend on education, family background, personality, experience, or competence for our confidence we are essentially depending on the flesh. Even though all of these are from God (1 Corinthians 4:7), when we depend on them alone we are depending on ourselves, not God. "The mind set on the flesh is hostile toward God. . . . Those who are in the flesh cannot please God" (Romans 8:7,8, NASB).

If we focus on our achievements and abilities we face disappointment, for they will eventually fade. They cannot last forever. We need to shift our focus from ourselves to God, from our attributes to God's attributes, from depending on our flesh to depending on God. Only He can give us true satisfaction and confidence.

We regain confidence by putting our confidence in God. Confidence in the flesh says, "Look what I have done," or "Look at who I am." God will not tolerate that arrogance. He insists that we find our fulfillment in Him, not in the world of accomplishments. He wants to root our confidence in His love and His grace.

QUESTIONS FOR THOUGHT AND DISCUSSION

1. What is confidence?

2. What are the root causes of loss of confidence?

3. What sources contribute to our own inherent confidence?

4. If we have placed too much confidence in education, family, or background, how can we *begin* to place confidence in God?

5. What are some ways you can choose to respond to loss of confidence?

SCRIPTURAL INSIGHTS:

1. What do 1 Corinthians 4:7 and Philippians 3:4-16 teach about confidence?

CHAPTER EIGHT

THE ANTIDOTE FOR LOSS

RECENTLY my wife Mary discovered a lump in her breast. She had experienced them before, so we approached the lumpectomy without much concern. The surgeon came out of the operating room saying that all looked fine but that he had ordered a routine biopsy. When the results came back we heard the dreaded word, cancer!

Suddenly life took on a different perspective. Consultations, reading, and discussions ensued to determine what should be done to cure or remove the cancer. We needed the right antidote—the best procedure. The treatment we chose eradicated the cancer to the best of our knowledge. Through the process we grew spiritually as we contemplated possible outcomes and losses.

Other friends have not been so fortunate. One friend has a cancer which the doctors simply do not know how to treat. Any chemotherapy is simply guesswork. Our friend chose a nutritional route of therapy.

In both cases the final outcome rests with God. The medicine and the antidote differ. Various cancers require specific cures, cures that are not speculative, but divinely set by God.

After delving into the many losses that overtake us when we least expect them, we now turn to practical and biblical cures. God knew us as men and as individuals before we were born. He knew the traumas that would intrude into our lives and He provided a cure.

Saul's Loss, Paul's Gain

Saul, the renegade Pharisee cum apostle, knew about loss. He had everything going for him in his work for the Jewish/Roman government. His family background was superb. He was born a high Jew as well as a Roman citizen. Educated under famed Gamaliel, he took his place in society as a Pharisee. He rapidly made a name for himself as a persecutor of people of "The Way"—believers in Christ. He excelled in tormenting Christians.

This Jesus was real. Paul had to choose between his known identity and Christ. The loss he felt did battle with the personal revelation of Jesus, the Truth.

Suddenly his bubble burst en route to Damascus. He was struck blind in a confrontation with Jesus. The voice said, "Saul, Saul, why do you persecute me?" Suspecting this was not a human interruption he asked, "Who are you, Lord?" "I am Jesus"(Acts 9:1-9). Impossible. Jesus is dead! Yet Jesus talked to him, demanding attention via Saul's blindness. Saul was ready to listen.

I can imagine Saul's fear. His confidence eroded. His background, education, identity, motivation, and influence no longer served to give him purpose. They disappeared in the blinding light that surrounded him. He feared Jesus and he feared his loss of identity. Paul was a man of integrity now faced with a difficult choice. This Jesus was real. Paul had to choose between his known identity and Christ. The loss he felt did battle with the personal revelation of Jesus, the Truth.

Later Saul, who became known as Paul (Acts 13:9), reflected on his loss. He recounted his roots and achievements as a means for confidence in the flesh: "circumcised the eighth day, of the nation of Israel, of the tribe of Benjamin, a Hebrew of the Hebrews; as to the Law, a Pharisee; as to zeal, a persecutor of the church; as to the righteousness which is in the Law, found blameless" (Philippians 3:5-6, NASB).

Paul assessed his loss:

> But whatever things were *gain* to me, these things I have counted as loss for the sake of Christ. More than that, I count all things to be loss in view of the surpassing value of knowing Christ Jesus my Lord, for whom I have suffered the loss of all things, and count them but rubbish in order that I may gain Christ, and may be found in Him, not having a righteousness of my own derived from the Law, but that which is through faith in Christ, the righteousness which comes from God on the basis of faith, that I may know Him, and the power of His resurrection and the fellowship of His sufferings, being conformed to His death. (Philippians 3:7-10, emphasis added)

The understanding of his loss did not come immediately. Paul was suffering for his newfound faith. He wrestled with the tradeoff. He probably wondered about his own sanity, as did the governor Festus when he expressed, "your great learning is driving you mad" (Acts 26:24). Paul knew he could not turn back from his encounter with Jesus. His conversion was genuine. He outlined the process of dealing with his loss:

1. He acknowledged his human inheritance and achievements.
2. He recognized them for what they were—useless rubbish.

3. He did not deny their importance nor their effect on his life. He remained grateful for them.
4. He saw his loss as the doorway to a new life in Christ.
5. His motivation was replaced with a motivation founded on knowing Christ and experiencing the power of that new life and relationship.

When Theory Penetrates Mind and Heart

At this point you may say, "Great theory. Been there, done that. Now what?"

Stop. You probably have not "been there, done that." This is not kindergarten material. This is the graduate school of human experience where the fundamentals of life take root.

> *Stop. You probably have not "been there, done that." This is not kindergarten material. This is the graduate school of human experience where the fundamentals of life take root.*

I clearly remember my graduate school experience when I studied Astronautics. Up to that time, I could pass tests, learn by rote, and give the right answers in my field. One professor started his class with the most basic concepts (of energy and mass) and rebuilt the theory. Lights flashed in my mind for the first time. I finally understood the "why" of what I had been using in my profession.

The same thing happens in the spiritual realm. Knowledge must be married to understanding *in* experience.

I observe two kinds of men.

The first is a man who has a personal relationship with Christ. He knows he has eternal life. When he is a young believer some of the biblical concepts are new. He needs to walk through them slowly, wrestling with ideas and considering their implications.

More mature believers (as I was in my personal losses) tend to skim over the concepts. Don't! This is the time for dissecting and rebuilding in spiritual graduate school. The truth needs to penetrate mind and heart.

The second kind of man is a man who is on the way to Christ. He is not certain that faith in Christ is the real answer to life. But he is open to the idea. He senses the frustrations of mediocre achievements. He has begun to feel their loss, their insignificance, and to look elsewhere for answers. He may have tried a number of substitutes to compensate for loss.

> *The key to living victoriously with loss is how I respond over time.*

Both types of men need deep and fundamental inner changes.

Keys to Responding to Loss

In dealing with losses in my own life I have learned one major lesson.

I cannot control my circumstance
But I can control my response.

Coming to this realization puts a major building block in place to rebuild the wounds of loss. The key to living victoriously with loss is HOW I RESPOND OVER TIME.

Note the two phrases: How I respond
Over time

Most of us cannot control our immediate response to any of these losses. It simply takes time to reflect on them, to understand our feelings about them and to reorder our thinking.

How I respond grows out of a series of realizations, concepts, and truths.

The most fundamental biblical truth is that *God is sovereign in all the circumstances of my life.* This means that God is all knowing and all controlling. This cannot be explained in human terms. It goes beyond our ability to comprehend. This truth is expressed in both Old and New Testaments.

See now that I myself am He!
There is no god besides me.
I put to death and I bring to life.
I have wounded and I will heal,
and no one can deliver out of my hand.
(Deuteronomy 32:39)

The LORD brings death and makes alive;
he brings down to the grave and raises up.
The Lord sends poverty and wealth;
he humbles and he exalts.
He raises the poor from the dust
and lifts the needy from the ash heap;
he seats them with princes
and has them inherit a throne of honor.
For the foundations of the earth are the LORD's;
upon them he has set the world. (1 Samuel 2:6-8)

God, the blessed and only Ruler, the King of kings and Lord
of lords, who alone is immortal and who lives in unapproach-
able light, whom no one has seen or can see. To him be
honor and might forever. Amen. (1 Timothy 6:15-16)

This is heavy theology, hard words. It is easier to talk of the love of
God or the love of Jesus. Not only is God sovereign, but fortunately
His sovereignty is expressed in complete love and compassion. He
knows our humanity and frailty.

Romans 8:35-39 expresses this truth in *The Message*. "I'm absolutely
convinced that nothing, absolutely nothing can get between us and
God's love because of the way that Jesus our Mentor embraced us."

The Antidote for Loss is Choosing to Grow

Though God is sovereign He never places us in circumstances without purpose and design. That leads to the foundational concept
that *this can be the time of greatest personal and spiritual growth in my*

life. It is through difficult circumstances that we grow. In many sports the saying "No pain, no gain" is often posted in full view of the athletes. Similarly, in the Christian life little growth occurs without discipline and pain.

Where's the Growth?

But how do we grow or how are we strengthened?

In Character. We grow in our inner person. We begin to develop those qualities of life that are most valuable—"love, joy, peace, patience, kindness, goodness, faithfulness, gentleness, and self-control" (Galatians 5:22-23).

The sad alternative is anger, bitterness, and resentment which lead to depression and deep loneliness. The middle ground between those two extremes is worse—a deadening of spirit, a refusal to feel, and a dying of life purpose.

In Choices. We choose. We choose our responses. At first it seems contrived or technical. Even the apostle Paul had to learn to respond properly. "I have learned to be content whatever the circumstance" (Philippians 4:11).

What do we choose?

1. We choose to believe that God is in control.
2. We choose to believe that everything we have is from God.

My intellect, my background, my abilities, my opportunities, and my achievements all come from God: Is there anything they would discover in you that you could take credit for? "Isn't everything you have and everything you are sheer gifts from God? So what's the point of all this comparing and competing? You already have all you need. You already have more access to God than you can handle" (1 Corinthians 4:7, MSG).

3. We choose to acknowledge our frailty and humanity.

Learn to count every day as a gift from God. Live for what is really important in life. One of the greatest lessons that came to me as a result of my son's death was the realization that what I had valued in an earthly sense was of little worth. Eternal values are paramount. Position, influence, and identity are as transient as a puff of breath on a frosty day. Momentarily visible, then gone.

4. We choose to examine our motives as related to our value system. Are the things that give you motivation and confidence really worthwhile? Are you depending on your position, identity, and influence for your self-worth?

5. We choose to rebuild our lives on a better foundation. That foundation is expressed by Paul: "I want to know Christ and the power of His resurrection" (Philippians 3:10). A desire to please and serve God, not ourselves, becomes our motive. To live for family and others, not ourselves.

In Training. The Bible refers to these losses as disciplines. They are not punishments, but training. As a master trainer or coach teaches us, so God trains us.

God disciplines His disciples in terms we understand as fathers—the discipline (not punishment) of our children for their good.

And you have forgotten that word of encouragement that addresses you as sons: "My son, do not make light of the Lord's discipline, and do not lose heart when he rebukes you," . . . Endure hardship as discipline; God is treating you as sons. For what son is not disciplined by his father? If you are not disciplined (and everyone undergoes discipline), then you are illegitimate children and not true sons. No discipline seems pleasant at the time, but painful. Later on, however, it produces a harvest of righteousness and peace for those who have been trained by it. (Hebrews 12:5,7-8,11)

God's Purpose in Loss

God's purpose is the "harvest of righteousness"—right living that pleases Him. Discipline produces a beautiful harvest of deep inner peace in our lives.

My friend and mentor J. Oswald Sanders endured and overcame much loss. Before he was fifty he was afflicted with arthritis so badly that he could hardly get out of bed. Here in the prime of his mid-life it appeared that he would be permanently physically limited. But he kept moving. He kept working. As he entered his second and third careers (principal of a Bible college and General Director of the China Inland Mission) he was totally freed from arthritis. He could have given up. He could have taken a nice retirement. Instead he entered into what many would say were the most procreative years of his life.

He wrote:

> The discipline is always preparatory to blessing and can bring nothing but blessing when rightly received. It is here that our responsibility lies. Food not digested is a bane, not a blessing. Disciplines not rightly received sour rather than sweeten the character. To querulously ask "Why?" when the chastening stroke falls is in effect to charge the all-wise and all-loving God with caprice. *He does not rend the heart merely to demonstrate His power and sovereignty but to prepare for greater fruitfulness.* He prunes every branch that does bear fruit to increase its yield. The discipline is purposeful. How do we react to God's plow? Does it soften, subdue, chasten us? Or does it harden and stiffen our resistance to his will? Does it sweeten or sour us? (emphasis added).[1]

He then says God has three purposes in the discipline:

- Personal, to cultivate the soul
- Relative, to provide food (blessing) to others
- Ultimate, to prepare (us) for heaven

He goes on to quote Alexander Whyte:

> We cease to wonder so much at the care God takes of human character and the cost He lays out upon it, when we think that it is the only work of His hands that shall last forever . . . riches, honor, possessions, pleasures of all kinds; death with one stroke of His desolate hand shall one day strip us bare to a winding sheet and a coffin of all the things we are so mad to possess.[2]

There is so much more to life. We must not allow temporal losses to detour us from becoming the best we can be in Christ. That is the unseen danger — that we fail to gain strength in loss, to respond with a learner's spirit, and to grow deeper in true character.

QUESTIONS FOR THOUGHT AND DISCUSSION

1. Have you experienced loss that caused detours in your life? What was the relationship between your decisions during those times and getting off track?

2. How can loss in life lead to a more intimate walk with Christ?

3. What happens when we believe we can control our circumstances and try to live on our own?

4. Do you believe that controlling your negative circumstances is within your power? Why, or why not?

5. How does a deep belief in God's sovereignty and purpose help us to withstand loss?

6. How does time give perspective needed to deal with loss?

7. How can periods of pain and loss be times of spiritual growth?

SCRIPTURAL INSIGHTS:

1. Consider Philippians 3 and 4. How does one learn contentment? What important things about God do we need to believe when we're experiencing loss?

THE DANGER
OF SIN

CHAPTER NINE

THE DANGER OF SIN

SIN. Such a cold word. Such a hard word. If we could just call sin a mistake, lapse of judgment, or a failure. We fear sin, but we are drawn irresistibly to it in so many areas of life. Consider these heroes of faith:

- Noah was a man who sinned in his old age.
- Samson was a man who sinned in his youth.
- David was a man who sinned in his success.
- Saul was a man who sinned in his pride.

Man after man in the Bible stumbled along the way. Few finished well. Men like Moses, Noah, and David were scattered among the wreckage of men who started well but succumbed to sin.

Sin overtook them and destroyed years of credibility. Of all dangers, sin is the most potent. It destroys, maims, and cripples.

> *In both pictures the prey is ignorant of the danger. All is well. Then suddenly, disaster strikes!*

The first brothers in human history, Cain and Abel, felt the disastrous impact of sin in their lives and family. Each came to God with an offering. Cain brought a grain offering. Abel brought an animal from his flock. God accepted Abel's offering but not Cain's. The Bible does not record the reason for God's displeasure with Cain's offering. Cain's problem may have been attitude or sincerity. Cain's response reflected what resided in his heart. "So Cain became very angry and his countenance fell" (Genesis 4:5, NASB). Anger gripped him. Discouragement infected his spirit.

God was not angry with Cain, but was trying to help him deal with problems of his heart.

> Then the LORD said to Cain, "Why are you angry? And why has your countenance fallen? If you do well, will not your countenance be lifted up? And if you do not do well, *sin is crouching at the door; and its desire is for you, but you must master it.*" (Genesis 4:6, NASB, emphasis added)

What a terrifying word picture. In Kenya, I have observed a lioness stalking her prey. She stops behind a bush. Her powerful legs bend, her body tenses to spring on her target and destroy it.

Peter uses a similar word picture: "Your adversary, the devil, prowls about like a roaring lion, seeking someone to devour" (1 Peter 5:8, NASB).

In both pictures *the prey is ignorant of the danger.* All is well. Then suddenly, disaster strikes!

The dangers addressed in this book are like that. Unexpected. Surprises. Without warning. Even though we are aware of the *possibility*, we cannot imagine it will happen to us. No matter how mature we are spiritually or chronologically, we are always vulnerable.

Before making any attempt to identify specific sins it is important to understand more about the biblical view of sin, its nature, and its power. Without such an understanding we might simply review the "nasty nine" or "filthy five" list of sins in an attempt to frighten ourselves sufficiently to keep us from committing them.

The Nature of Sin

It is helpful to know the "whys" of the admonition to do or not to do something. As a young believer I was given prohibitions to avoid alcohol, dancing, movies, smoking, and other activities. I was aware that some Christians thought these activities were sins. I did not know the biblical basis for their reasoning. The effect was to engender confusion regarding the seriousness of sin.

The key to overcoming these problems resides in the crucified life.

Most of us have the desire expressed in Psalm 119:133. "Direct my footsteps according to your word; let no sin rule over me." No man wants to allow sin to rule or dominate him. We want a clear conscience and a pure heart.

As we work toward the goal of a life free from the bondage of sin we need to more fully understand the nature of sin. Two issues seem to plague every thinking believer in Christ:

1. A lack of commitment that lasts for a lifetime
2. The discouragement of sins that seem to persist in our lives

Overcoming Sin
The key to overcoming these problems resides in the crucified life. It is summarized in Galatians 2:20-21:

I have been crucified with Christ and I no longer live, but Christ lives in me. The life I live in the body, I live by faith in the Son of God, who loved me and gave himself for me. I do not set aside the grace of God, for if righteousness could be gained through the law, Christ died for nothing!

This truth is reinforced in Romans 6:6-7: "For we know that our old self was crucified with him so that the body of sin might be done away with, that we should no longer be slaves to sin—because anyone who has died has been freed from sin."

We live with the dilemma of sin. Clearly we are no longer under the law, attempting to please God by our good deeds. We are under grace. Our salvation comes by grace through faith. We do not earn it. We are saved from the penalty of sin. The dilemma is, "Why do I keep on sinning?"

Why Do We Keep Sinning?

A thorough study of Romans 5 and 6 answers this question. In Romans 4, Paul recounted the experience of Abraham—particularly how he received his salvation by grace, not by works. When Abraham trusted God to fulfill His promise to provide a son as an heir, "this is why it was credited to him as righteousness" (see Genesis 15).

The words "it was credited to him" were written not for him alone, but also for us, to whom God will credit righteousness—for we who believe in Him who raised Jesus our Lord from the dead. He was delivered over to death for our sins and was raised to life for our justification.

Therefore, since we have been justified through faith, we have peace with God through our Lord Jesus Christ, through whom we have gained access by faith into this grace in which we now stand. (Romans 4:22–5:1)

We need to look at this passage as an attorney would look at a contract, examining every word and phrase. The key concepts are:

- We receive God's unearned favor (grace) when we place our faith (believe) in Christ and His death for our sins, and His victory over death in resurrection.

- We are then *justified* (righteousness credited to our
  account). This is a legal term meaning that the debt or
  charges against us are totally erased and forgiven.
- We have peace with God—no debt remaining to be paid.
- Our residence (where we stand) is "in Christ." We are
  totally under the roof of His protection.

We have no further penalty to pay for our sin. It has been fully paid
by Christ in His death on the cross for our sin. Therefore, even
though we are now dead to sin in terms of its future power over us,
we are still susceptible to its presence and *influence*.

The Power of Sin Shattered
At this point we need to contrast sin (singular) and sins (plural):

> Therefore, just as sin (singular) entered the world through
> one man (Adam) and death through sin (singular), and this
> way death came to all men, because all sinned—for before
> the law was given, sin was in the world (through Adam's sin).
> . . . Consequently, just as the result of one trespass was con-
> demnation for all men, so also the result of one act of right-
> eousness was justification that brings life for all men.
> (Romans 5:12-13,18; parentheses added)

The external power of sin and the penalty of sin have been forever
shattered. The old self died with Christ. We are now a new creation
(2 Corinthians 5:17). The result of this death is twofold:

1. Our new life here and our resurrection to eternal life are
   assured. We are free from the penalty of sin. *Sin shall not
   be your master.* Satan's power is broken.
2. We *should no longer be slaves to sin.* Sin no longer has
   legal power over us. But we still need to choose to be free.

Even though we are free, we can choose to live as slaves. Sin lost its
power over us, but sins and sinning still plague our human lives. Our

old self died with Christ, but our fleshly human nature still lives. Before we came to faith in Christ we did not have the power to resist sin. The power of Christ living in us now gives us every resource we need to resist a life of sinning. Romans 6:11 says: "Count yourselves dead to sin." That means that we are now to act on the reality that our old self is dead.

Freedom from Sin

Picture yourself in a prison cell on death row, having been sentenced to death. A judge suddenly pardons you and orders your freedom. The cell doors open. But you decide to stay in prison. You are free. You will not be executed. But you do not leave and exercise your freedom. This is the picture of a believer who is free, but chooses to continue letting sins invade his life.

> *Even though we are free, we can choose to live as slaves.*

The Living Bible paraphrases Romans 6:11: "So look upon your old sin nature as dead and unresponsive to sin, and instead be alive to God, alert to him, through Jesus Christ our Lord."

Act on the fact! The phrase "live in reality" reflects this truth. We all know of men who live in a dream world. But many men live in a nightmare world of captivity to sin. The nightmare is not real, but we can act as though it were, which leads to fear and incapacity. We need to act on truth—the truth that we have died to sin in Christ. That is our position. We now need to live in accordance with our position as sons of God.

We are like the multimillion dollar lottery winner who has the choice of continuing to live as a pauper or to use the wealth to bring himself out of poverty.

We still need to fully answer the question, "Why do I keep on sinning if I have died to sin?" Sin no longer possesses unbreakable power over us, but it still is a powerful force. I still have the propensity and the ability to sin. If I did not, why would 1 John 1:9-10 be such key verses for believers? "If we confess our sins, he is faithful and just and will forgive us our sins and purify us from all unrighteousness. If we claim we have not sinned, we make him out to be a liar and his word has no place in our lives."

Once again, we see the concept of sin and sins: "You have been set free from sin . . . and the result is eternal life" (Romans 6:22). This being the case, "Therefore, do not let sin reign in your mortal body so that you obey its evil desires" (Romans 6:12). We now have a choice. Before salvation we had no choice—we followed sin blindly. As believers we possess the power of the Holy Spirit to make godly choices in spite of the flesh and our sinful nature that will plague us until physical death. We are freed from the penalty of sin but we are not free from the influence of sins. Our choices:

- Serve sin—in the flesh
- Serve righteousness—in the Spirit

In chapter fourteen, I will discuss the practical application of these truths in living a Spirit-led life. First, let's consider four of the unexpected dangers of sin which can so easily sneak up on men like a lion stalking its prey.

QUESTIONS FOR THOUGHT AND DISCUSSION

1. Why does no amount of maturity, wisdom, age, experience, knowledge, or position make us immune to temptation?

2. What does it mean to finish well? Why does it seem hard to do? How does sin creep in and keep us from finishing the race well?

3. What circumstances make you particularly vulnerable to sin *that is crouching at the door*?

4. What practical steps can you take, or have you taken, to lower your exposure to those things which make you more vulnerable?

5. What are you doing right now to help you finish well?

SCRIPTURAL INSIGHTS:

1. Consider Romans 6. If we are *dead to sin*, why do we still sin?

2. How does being dead to sin influence our freedom and decision making on a daily basis?

3. What does it mean to *count yourselves dead to sin* and how do we act on this reality in our lives?

CHAPTER TEN

WHEN SEXUAL TEMPTATION BECOMES SIN

*A prudent man sees danger and takes refuge,
but the simple keep going and suffer for it.*
PROVERBS 22:3

O<small>NE</small> of my friends, Cliff, had been moving toward Christ for a number of years. Several times he was almost ready to commit his life to Christ. He told me, "I started going to church. Then the pastor ran off with the organist. It seemed that every time I reached a place where I trusted a Christian they did some dumb thing like that, so I backed off."

We all know more stories like that than we care to recount. Yet, even as we observe others fall, we think we are immune. We are not. Disaster can strike any of us. We live with the danger described in Proverbs 22:3: "A prudent man sees danger and takes refuge, but the simple keep going and suffer for it." We see it and keep going, and suffer greatly for it.

Many of you reading this book have a past, or even a present, sexual sin. You may be trapped by an addiction to illicit sex, pornography, or some other sexual sin. Don't despair or skip this chapter if you have tried many times and failed to overcome your sin.

There is a way out. God forgives completely. There is no sin He does not forgive. No persistent or habitual sin loosens its hold easily. That is what these next chapters are all about.

What is Temptation?

We would all agree that sexual immorality is sin. But what about sexual activities of mind and body short of immorality? What do we do with sexual temptations?

We are all tempted. All men struggle with sexual temptation. "The lust of the flesh and the lust of the eyes" (1 John 2:16, NASB) draw us like magnets.

What is temptation? Some synonyms for "tempt" are allure, attract, entice, seduce, and tantalize. Some synonyms for "tempted" are: enchanted, entranced, bewitched, hypnotized, spellbound, charmed, mesmerized, enraptured, and captivated. Each word generates an emotional picture. Temptation relates to sin. Men are allured by it. We are attracted to it, enticed by it, seduced by its seeming pleasure, tantalized by the fantasy of what it would be like. We experience sexual temptation daily. It is our plague, our persistent sickness.

Sex is the ultimate risk for men when they choose to violate its scriptural use in the context of marriage.

If I were writing this book to women, would I include sexual temptation as a major danger? Yes, but not in the same way. Women certainly are tempted sexually. Sexual immorality does take two. But the drive and the motive are different. According to Robert Hicks in *The Masculine Journey*, it is not the hourly frontal lobe preoccupation for most women as it is for most men. Women generally want intimacy, communication, and relationship in the context of security and family.[1]

Men are easily driven to excessive behavior. This drive is focused primarily on sex, power, and money—probably in that order. Power over people, circumstances, their own lives, their wives and children all express this drive.

Money becomes a persistent force throughout a man's life. He rarely has enough. Whether wealthy or not, a man pushes to make money. Sometimes it is simply to provide for his family. Often it is to provide a sense of worth and security. Both money and power obsessions can lead to sin.

The Ultimate Risk for Men

But sex and sexual temptation fall into a class all their own. Sex is the ultimate risk for men when they choose to violate its scriptural use in the context of marriage.

Robert Hicks describes one major aspect of man in the Hebrew word structure as the Phallic man (the Hebrew, *eakur*, is a name for the male in terms of his male sex organ—penis or phallus). He comments, "Many men get stuck in Phallic City, though it is a normal part of developing manhood. It begins in adolescence and continues throughout the life span."[2]

Sexual Temptation Starts in the Mind

Sexual temptation is *not* primarily physical. It begins in the mind. In another book I wrote, I noted:

> Sexual sin never begins by accident. People do not suddenly fall into an illicit sexual act simply by having an opportunity confront them. There is always some specific preparation. This preparation we call "pre-sexual" experience. Pre-sexual experiences are those experiences of mind and action which excite, train, or develop our sexual drives.[3]

Sexual temptation is an issue of the mind. The mind can only act on what has confronted it through sight, reading, or hearing. Therefore, to guard against sexual temptation we must be careful what we look at, read, or listen to. Images are planted which cause lust to take hold. Even when we do not act out immorality we can be polluted by a mental and emotional fixation on sex.

The Power of Porn

Pornography in its many forms can so easily get a foothold in our lives. Hicks writes:

> The real power of pornography is that it provides men with the ultimate fantasy fulfillment without the risk of emotional rejection that often accompanies relationship with "real" women. In normal sexual relations, our fragile male egos are on the line, and often the slightest rejection of our advances can drive us quickly into seclusion, brooding, and hurt. Pornography solves the problem. There exists a seemingly unceasing supply of super attractive, inviting women, always available, always willing—and who give the impression that each reader (viewer) is very special. *Pornographic literature plays with our minds at the deepest levels* (emphasis added).[4]

Pornography does not just hinder us, it destroys us. Our walk with God is hindered by images which will not leave us. The danger is that it starts with minor indiscretions, seemingly harmless. Then it tantalizes us until we are caught in its web. Some of you know firsthand the despair, guilt, and helplessness that come with this practice.

Pornography is inextricably linked to masturbation for most men. In spite of the blessing the secular world gives to this practice, declaring it as normal, we know that it connects to poisonous sexual images in our minds. Masturbation feeds on visual images to excite us. An excellent book to help men struggling with masturbation is *The War Within . . . Experiencing Victory in the Battle for Sexual Purity* by Robert Daniels.[5]

A few months after our son was murdered, Mary and I were on a ministry trip to Thailand. Close friends, Ed and Merrilee Turley, asked us to go with them for three days to a resort on the coast. It was an incredibly beautiful setting.

Cottages were perched on a lush hillside above the beach. A small sand beach was nestled in the rocks about one hundred feet below the cottages.

Late the first afternoon, I decided to go for a short swim. The beach area was deserted. I swam about one hundred feet out, enjoying the tropical waters. I turned to swim to the shore and found I was caught in an outflowing current and could not make any headway toward land. I imagined being swept out to sea. I knew enough to swim parallel to the beach toward the rocky curve of the inlet. But the sea bottom was coral. I stumbled out after cutting my legs and hands on the coral. Thankfully I made it.

At dinner that night I sheepishly told our friends what had happened. A strange smile crossed Ed's face. He said, "The same thing happened to me about half an hour before it happened to you." He had to call out and a life guard came to help him.

That experience mirrors what sexual temptation does to us. It looks so pleasant and enjoyable. Then we get caught in its grip. We struggle to get out but are ensnared and bruised in the process. We often do not see the real danger until it is too late.

I didn't swim in that cove again!

The Sources of Sexual Temptation

What causes this temptation? It comes from Satan and our flesh. "When tempted, no one should say, 'God is tempting me.' For God cannot be tempted by evil, nor does he tempt anyone; but each one is tempted when, by his own evil desire, he is dragged away and enticed" (James 1:13-14).

Remember, the sinful nature died with Christ. It no longer has irresistible power over us. We can choose—and must choose. Temptation is placed before us, but by the Holy Spirit we possess the power to withstand it.

That is the teaching of 1 Corinthians 10:13: "No temptation has seized you except what is common to man. And God is faithful; he will not let you be tempted beyond what you can bear. But when you are tempted, he will also provide a way out so that you can stand up under it."

Temptation is the common experience of all men, but God always provides a way out. However, note the verse just prior to this: "So, if you think you are standing firm, be careful that you don't fall" (1 Corinthians 10:12). We are vulnerable. We must be on the alert. This command is in the imperative voice . . . take heed, watch out, be careful!

Principles for Dealing with Sexuality

Several years ago I took a number of our Navigator leadership couples on a four day whitewater rafting trip down the Green River in Utah. It was an amazingly beautiful wilderness area in the Dinosaur National Monument. Each night we slept in tents along the river. Just before leaving on this trip I found out that a friend, a Christian leader known to many of us, had publicly confessed to sexual sin. I was greatly troubled. In spite of the pristine beauty of the place, the clear air and the relaxing atmosphere, I couldn't sleep. In the middle of the night, I took my flashlight and walked out from the camp, sat down, and wrote the following letter to the men on my newsletter list.

An Important Letter

Dear friends,

As I lay awake for about three hours one night in June, I felt personally burdened to share some thoughts with the men on our newsletter list. This is neither a newsletter nor a prayer letter, but rather a simple expression of some ideas that I hope will stimulate your thinking.

In view of some recent events, I think we need to honestly discuss the issue of sexual purity. I am addressing men since I am a man and can only speak from that perspective. But as women read this letter, it will help them understand the issues from a man's viewpoint.

Sexual purity is a direct command of Scripture. "For this is the will of God, your sanctification; that is, that you abstain from sexual immorality" (1 Thessalonians 4:3, NASB). There are no excuses. Repentance, yes. Forgiveness, yes. Excuses, no. And for some reason, the results of sexual sin, though sins are not graded by God, seem much more far reaching.

Here are some principles . . . thoughts . . . observations:

1. Sexual sin is always generated in the mind before it is acted out in the body. Thus, to guard one's thoughts is absolutely indispensable.
2. A struggling marriage is never an excuse for sexual sin.
3. A widowed, divorced person, or sexually-experienced man will likely have more temptation, mainly due to knowledge.
4. In cases I have seen, some common threads emerge and seem characteristic of men who have fallen into sexual impurity:

   - The macho image and a sense of dominance.
   - A perceived failure in one's job or a blow to one's ego or pride.
   - A feeling of being "above the rules."
   - Going easy on one's self . . . in many areas like diet or exercise.
   - Carelessly allowing one's self to be in places or situations that boost temptation.
   - A roving and undisciplined eye.

5. Accountability is a major key to prevention, though not the only answer.
6. Even with accountability, one who wants to sin sexually will find a way to lie and deceive others, and himself, to avoid the truth. Thus, we must uphold one another with prayer.
7. Regardless of spiritual maturity or chronological age or the best of marriages, everyone is vulnerable to sexual sin.

How can I have accountability? I suggest having someone ask you direct questions at least periodically—perhaps monthly. Here are some possibilities:

1. Are you involved sexually with anyone other than your wife?
2. Are you using pornography?
3. Are you masturbating? (This is certainly a controversial issue. I suggest you examine the chapter on sexual morality in my book *Honesty, Morality and Conscience.* Many believe that masturbation is not a serious issue. I tend to view it differently.)
4. Are you watching "R" or "X" rated movies or videos?
5. Are you indulging in sexual fantasies about other women?

But after all of this, we might ask, "What are some of the best preventative measures against sexual sin?" Here are some suggestions:

1. Daily time with God in His Word and a commitment to spiritual growth.
2. A commitment to the battle for winning the lost.
3. A committed accountability relationship with one or two other men.
4. A deepening marriage relationship with your wife.
5. A constant guard in your thought life and actions.
6. Determined and continually renewed commitment that you will not enter into sexual sin.
7. Defensive prayer.

Chuck Swindoll in his book *Growing Strong in the Seasons of Life* made some insightful comments regarding David and Solomon:

> *Deterioration is never sudden.* No garden suddenly "overgrows" with thorns. No church suddenly "splits." No building suddenly "crumbles." No marriage suddenly "breaks down." No nation suddenly becomes a "mediocre

power." No person suddenly "becomes base." Slowly, almost imperceptibly, certain things are accepted that once were rejected. Things once considered hurtful are now secretly tolerated. At the outset it appears harmless, perhaps even exciting, but the wedge it brings leaves a gap that grows wider as moral erosion joins hands with spiritual decay. The gap becomes a canyon. That "way which seems right" becomes, in fact, "the way of death." Solomon wrote that. He ought to know.

Take heed, you who stand: take heed lest *you* fall! Be careful about changing your standards so that they correspond with your desires. Be very cautious about becoming inflated with thoughts of your own importance. Be alert to the pitfalls of prosperity and success. Should God grant riches, fame, and success, don't run scared or feel guilty. Just stay balanced. Remember Solomon, who deteriorated from a humble man of wisdom to a vain fool in a rather brief span of time.[6]

Yours in Christ,

Dr. Jerry White

Note: Please feel free to reproduce and distribute this letter.
Please reference this book as its source.

In these intervening years, thousands of copies of that letter have been reproduced and read in men's groups. Why? Because everyone recognizes his vulnerability and sincerely wants to prevent a fall.

The Motivation Behind the Principles

What is our motivation? You will likely say, "Fear!" Fear is a strong motivator. Fear God and keep His commands. "It is a fearful thing to fall into the hands of the living God" (Hebrew 10:31, NASB).

Fear is not enough. Fear works well only when there is an immediate consequence. "When the sentence for a crime is not quickly carried out, the hearts of the people are filled with schemes to do wrong" (Ecclesiastes 8:11).

Often we practice sexual activities short of immorality and observe that life seems to go on. Where is God? When will I be found out? When will the lightning strike? Like tentatively stepping into cold water on a beach, we soon get used to it and venture deeper toward danger. So, too, we go deeper as we give in to sexual temptation. Fear is a temporary stopgap measure, a warning.

The primary motivation is that we are the image of Christ and we do not want to stain that image. We want to live a pure and holy life. We want to be slaves of righteousness, not slaves to sin.

"You have been set free from sin and have become slaves to righteousness" (Romans 6:18). In his classic discussion of sexual immorality, Paul classifies the motivation: "Do you not know that your body is a temple of the Holy Spirit, who is in you, whom you have received from God? You are not your own; you were bought at a price. Therefore honor God with your body" (1 Corinthians 6:19,20).

In the Old Testament, Israel often abandoned God; He likened them to women prostituting themselves sexually to other gods. Much of the worship of false gods included immorality with temple prostitutes. God *always* held them accountable.

Most men I know really do want to please God, to live a pure and holy life. They hate the habits of mind and body that capture them. They want release. That release is available. It comes through confession, repentance, forgiveness, and spiritual renewal.

Guidelines for Handling Temptations

I was looking out the window of my house one day, and saw a simple-minded lad, a young man lacking common sense, walking at twilight down the street to the house of this wayward girl, a prostitute. She approached him, saucy and pert and dressed seductively. She was the brash, coarse type, seen often in the streets and markets, soliciting at every corner for men to be her lovers.

She put her arms around him and kissed him, and with a saucy look she said, "I was just coming to look for you and here you are! My bed is spread with lovely, colored sheets of finest linen imported from Egypt, perfumed with myrrh, aloes, and cinnamon. Come on, let's take our fill of love until morning, for my husband is away on a long trip. He has taken a wallet full of money with him and won't return for several days.

So she seduced him with her pretty speech, her coaxing and her wheedling, until he yielded to her. He couldn't resist her flattery. He followed her as an ox going to the butcher, or as a stag that is trapped, waiting to be killed with an arrow through its heart. He was as a bird flying into a snare, not knowing the fate awaiting it there.

Listen to me, young men, and not only listen but obey; don't let your desires get out of hand; don't let yourself think about her. Don't go near her; stay away from where she walks, lest she tempt you and seduce you. For she has been the ruin of multitudes—a vast host of men have been her victims. If you want to find the road to hell, look for her house. (Proverbs 7:6-27, TLB)

This description of a foolish man entrapped by sexual temptation strikes close to home for so many of us. It sends fear through our minds, bringing on susceptibility. What can we do? How can we escape the traps that appear before us?

Several guidelines for dealing with sexual temptations emerge from this passage:

1. Don't let your desires get out of hand . . . control them.
2. Don't let yourself think about her . . . guard your mind.
3. Don't go near her . . . run from tempting circumstances.
4. Guard your eyes, what you see—movies, photographs, or other women. "I made a covenant with my eyes not to look lustfully at a girl" (Job 31:1).

Our marriages and our lives are at stake. We ought to fear the consequences, for they are great. We need to cut the temptation at its root to prevent its devouring impact on our life.

You may be saying, "It's too late. I've already given in to sexual temptation. My marriage is broken or disintegrating. What do I do now?" God is a God of compassion and forgiveness. He can and will still intervene, if you give Him permission. He can rebuild what has been torn down. God is willing and ready to work on your behalf.

None of us can escape sexual temptation. It is a fact of life. And men who claim to follow Christ will want to live a life of purity. We cannot do it on our own. We need God's help to live this life of victory.

QUESTIONS FOR THOUGHT AND DISCUSSION

1. What circumstances produce the greatest level of vulnerability to sexual temptation in your life?
2. What role does accountability play in your battle for sexual purity?
3. If you have had exposure to or have struggled with pornography in the past, are there one or two other men who are aware of this and keep you accountable in this area?
4. Robert Hicks is quoted as saying that *pornographic literature plays with our minds at its deepest levels.* Why and how is this true?
5. If sexual sin begins in the mind, what steps can you take to deal with this issue in your thought life?
6. Are there other areas of sin you are not dealing with or issues in your conscience you are ignoring? How does sin in other areas affect your ability to resist sexual temptation? What happens when we compartmentalize things in our minds and hearts?

SCRIPTURAL INSIGHTS:

1. Consider Romans 7. What can you learn from this passage about sexual temptation?

WHEN CONFLICT BECOMES SIN

MEN are made "more for combat than comfort," writes Elliot Engel in a commentary on men's friendships.[1] Competition and conflict seem to suit men. Conflict is the norm in the business world. Conflict over ideas, strategies, concepts, methods, and decisions are part of every man's job experience.

We evaluate, discuss, and compromise. Some men handle this environment of competition for ideas very well, while others shrivel inwardly and develop ulcers.

When Conflict Becomes Dangerous

Conflict is normal within certain boundaries. Discussion, dialogue, and constructive criticism comprise positive elements of our conversations.

We cross that boundary when emotions flare. Anger deepens and personal tension enters relationships. Even then, conflict can be constructive. We may not have crossed the boundary, but if another person does, tension mounts. It is healthy to recognize it and deal with it. Unacknowledged and left to simmer, conflict becomes a poison to our lives. When is conflict a sign of danger to a man?

- When the conflict is a repeated pattern in your life.
- When many or most conflicts remain unresolved.
- When you sense a pattern of unwillingness to be open to other positions or thinking.

Men engage in conflict easily but find it difficult to resolve. Conflict is often a way of life in work and business. When conflict carries over to our marriage and friendships it becomes very destructive.

Paul, the feisty apostle, who had his own share of conflict, wrote:

> For I am afraid that when I come I may not find you as I want you to be, *and you may not* find me as you want me to be. I fear that there may be quarreling, jealousy, outbursts of anger, factions, slander, gossip, arrogance, and disorder. (2 Corinthians 12:20)

He saw his own friends from Corinth in conflict—and in sin. He both warns them and encourages them to be at peace. We know that conflict is a seedbed for a multitude of moral sins. As men, we cannot let conflict pollute and spoil us.

The Roots of Conflict

Conflict differs from simple disagreement, debate, or discussion in that it springs from a root of sin. "He who loves a quarrel loves sin" (Proverbs 17:19). The strongest statements on simple conflict come from Galatians 5:19-21: "The acts of the sinful nature are obvious: sexual immorality, impurity and debauchery; idolatry and witchcraft; hatred, discord, jealousy, fits of rage, selfish ambition, dissensions, factions and envy; drunkenness, orgies, and the like."

We can easily agree with the first five sins in the list, but the next eight are more easily overlooked. To our human minds they seem too mild to be included with the first five. But God takes them seriously. Notice the last part of verse 21: "I warn you as I did before, that those who live like this will not inherit the kingdom of God."

Discord, dissension, and factions form the heart of conflict. Unfortunately, conflict comes so naturally to men. Robert Hicks describes man in one major element of his character — as Warrior. He describes the root Hebrew word, *gibbor*, with the "idea of gaining the upper hand."[2] He further says that "As men we war in business, in sports, in marriage, in our conversations, and with our political agendas."[3] That is the essence of conflict — to win. We want precisely that in war — a warrior who wins. In the normal conduct of life such an attitude becomes tiresome and unpalatable.

> *That is the essence of conflict — to win. We want precisely that in war — a warrior who wins. In the normal conduct of life such an attitude becomes tiresome and unpalatable.*

Conflict is one of the prime evidences of sinful worldliness. "You are still worldly. For since there is jealousy and quarreling among you, are you not worldly? Are you not acting like mere men?" (1 Corinthians 3:3).

You may wonder why I include conflict as an unseen or unexpected danger. I do so because of its profoundly destructive power on individuals and the community. I also include it because it is so hard for a man to either admit he is wrong in a conflict or admit that conflict is a harmful pattern in his life.

The Results of Conflict

Individual conflict is the first source of group conflict. Throughout the Bible, conflict and dissension caused murder, wars, division of families, and struggles for power.

In the church body, more difficulties surface from conflict than from doctrinal disagreement. When churches fail to grow and the lost are not being reached, at the root you will find internal conflict among the leadership.

The result of conflict in the individual man is manifold. Conflict leads to *anger*, both internal and external.

Conflict destroys *friendships* and *working relationships*. The Bible says, "An evil man sows strife; gossip separates the best of friends" (Proverbs 16:28, TLB). Unresolved conflict puts a wedge between friends. It prevents peace and unity which is highly valued in the Scripture. "If you keep on biting and devouring each other, watch out or you will be destroyed by each other" (Galatians 5:15). Prolonged conflict is the antithesis of love.

Conflict causes *spiritual weakness* and *immaturity*. Isaiah wrote of a striking contrast between spiritual fasting and quarreling:

> For day after day they seek me out; they seem eager to
> know my ways . . . eager for God to come near them. . . .
> Yet on the day of your fasting, you do as you please and
> exploit all your workers. Your fasting ends in quarreling
> and strife, and in striking each other with wicked fists. You
> cannot fast as you do today and expect your voice to be
> heard on high. (Isaiah 58:2-4)

The Living Bible paraphrases 1 Corinthians 3:3, highlighting this same truth:

> For you are still only baby Christians, controlled by your
> own desires, not God's. When you are jealous of one another
> and divide up into quarreling groups, doesn't that prove you
> are still babies, wanting your own way? In fact, you are acting
> like people who don't belong to the Lord at all.

Jesus instructs us first to be reconciled with our brother before offering spiritual sacrifices since we cannot have intimate fellowship with God when we are in a state of conflict (Matthew 5:24).

The result of conflict in a community of believers is disunity and dissension. This is a sad witness to the nonbelieving world. Conflicts in the Christian family lead to divisions and rifts in relationships that may last for a lifetime. Men and women everywhere are deeply wounded by such conflict.

The Way Out of Conflict

Although it is true that it takes two or more people to engender open conflict, examine yourself to see if you fall into a pattern of creating and fostering conflict.

What is the source of conflict? According to Proverbs 13:10, pride is one primary source of conflict.

Another is sinful desires:

What causes fights and quarrels among you? Don't they come from your desires that battle within you? You want something but don't get it. You kill and covet, but you cannot have what you want. You quarrel and fight. You do not have, because you do not ask God. When you ask, you do not receive, because you ask with wrong motives, that you may spend it on your pleasures. (James 4:1-3)

The root of conflict is in our inner person—a selfishness and pride that offends God and others.

If you find this pattern of conflict significantly in your life, there is a way out. There are good action steps you can take.

1. Confess this pattern to God. He already knows it, but confession is an admission of your need and a cry for help to God. Men find it so difficult to admit need, even privately to God.
2. Identify the major conflicts outstanding in your life. Write them down. Putting them on a piece of paper brings a new reality to them. It is also a reminder when you later may try to rationalize them away.
3. Begin a process of forgiveness and reconciliation. This will take time. You may need to forgive or be forgiven. Psalm 32:1 in the Living Bible describes the relief of

forgiveness. "What happiness for those whose guilt has been forgiven! What joys when sins are covered over! What relief for those who have confessed their sins and God has cleared their record." In the next few verses it tells how silence can make us physically ill and how peace relieves when forgiveness is active. In each case you may need to ask or give forgiveness. Reconciliation is not quite so easy. It takes two people. It is a process that also takes work and time. I recommend Ken Sande's book, *The Peacemaker*.[4] It outlines in detail how to bring about reconciliation.

4. In the future use the technique of Proverbs 20:3: "It is to a man's honor to avoid strife, but every fool is quick to quarrel." Don't let yourself enter the conflict, knowing your tendencies. Proverbs 17:14 confirms this thought: "Starting a quarrel is like breaching a dam; so drop the matter before a dispute breaks out." That old saying, "An ounce of prevention is worth a pound of cure," applies so well. You cannot totally avoid or prevent conflict, but there is so much you can do to make sure you are not the instigator.

5. Ask God to deal with root issues of pride and selfishness in your life. They are there for all of us. I find them constantly rearing their ugly heads in my own life. Particularly in my home I find that pride and selfishness engender conflicts between Mary and me. I seem to control it better with others, but they are still there. For some of us, we have never dealt with these root issues in a definitive way. It is a humbling, but necessary, experience. I have also found that I do not initiate dealing with them myself, that God takes His surgical knife and does it in a very public and humiliating way. God simply will not tolerate it for long.

6. Most of us enter conflict in the midst of our conversations with others. Thus we need to learn to guard our tongue— and our heart reactions. The biblical letter of James talks bluntly about the tongue: "If anyone considers himself

religious and yet does not keep a tight rein on his tongue, he deceives himself and his religion is worthless. . . . Likewise the tongue is a small part of the body, but it makes great boasts. Consider what a great forest is set on fire by a small spark. The tongue also is a fire, a world of evil among the parts of the body. It corrupts the whole person, sets the whole course of his life on fire, and is itself set on fire by hell" (James 1:26; 3:5-6). We need to treat our tendency to be in conflict at two levels. The first level is in what we say and how we say it. The second is in our heart and emotions. Our personality often governs our reactions, but they can be controlled and changed by God's work in our lives.

Finally we need to take full responsibility for our own actions, doing all that we can to curb and cure conflict. "If it is possible, as far as it depends on you, live at peace with everyone" (Romans 12:18).

As men, we know that stress is one of the major contributors to health problems and to our personal well-being. I believe that conflict is the major contributor to this stress for many men. Even on those of us who think we handle conflict well, it takes its inevitable toll.

QUESTIONS FOR THOUGHT AND DISCUSSION

1. Why is conflict a more subtle danger than other forms of more blatant sin or temptation?

2. When does disagreement or difference of opinion become strife and conflict that is sinful?

3. How does unresolved conflict affect individuals and the body of Christ?

4. How can conflict sometimes be a product of holding on too tightly to our own ideas and perspectives?

5. Is compromise a virtue and a sign of maturity or a weakness?

Explain. Are you able to compromise with others when necessary regarding goals, ideas, and desires?

6. Do you value unity above being right or having your way?

7. Why is resolving outstanding conflicts so crucial in your relationship to God?

8. As you look at previous conflicts in your life, do you tend to initiate reconciliation, wait for the other party to do so, or simply ignore it?

9. In a given conflict, we may be a legitimately injured party and believe we have the "high ground" in a claim against the offending party. Can you forgive someone who has wronged you and hold onto your rights at the same time? How does insistence upon "my way" stifle spiritual growth?

SCRIPTURAL INSIGHTS:

1. Consider Matthew 18. Whose responsibility is it to resolve conflict between two parties?

2. Compare the fruit of the Spirit in Galatians 5:22-23 with Galatians 5:19-21. In this context, how serious is conflict? How can it be overcome?

3. In Philippians 2:1-4, what are high values with God?

CHAPTER TWELVE

WHEN ANGER BECOMES SIN

I play handball. Perhaps I should say I *still* play handball. That admission in itself, I am told by friends, is enough to commit me to some category of instability or craziness. As in most competitive sports I see a lot of anger. In frustration men slam their fists into the wall, swear at themselves, or argue over a shot or a foul. Usually their temper is their undoing in a game. Only a very few play the game better when they are angry.

Most of us who play handball tolerate some degree of anger in others and in ourselves. But there are some people with whom no one likes to play. Their temper and conduct on the court are unbearable and inexcusable. I have seen yelling matches that are just short of physical blows. There are some who become sullen and give up, ruining the game by not playing to the best of their ability.

When the game is over they leave in their business suits and go back to being a lawyer, teacher, engineer, businessman, or stockbroker—seemingly normal people.

Conflict, anger, and pride intertwine inextricably. . . . they form a trilogy of dangers that subvert maturity, personal growth, and meaningful relationships.

Emotional boundaries exist even in a game. Frustration, anger, or disappointment with oneself or discouragement over errors are certainly legitimate. But the line is crossed when anger overtakes and controls. Then everyone becomes uncomfortable. Angry outbursts cause the person to lose respect whether or not he wins or loses the game.

So it is in life. Anger, out of bounds, never brings approval.

Certainly anger is not just a male emotion. Men and women alike possess and express anger. But they handle it differently. In the ongoing discussion over the differences in men's and women's communication and expression of feelings, there is the repeated frustration that men do not express their emotions. Anger is the only consistent emotion that men do express. Men's anger usually comes explosively rather than out of early communication that signals building anger.

Conflict, anger, and pride intertwine inextricably. I am discussing them separately because they form a trilogy of dangers that subvert maturity, personal growth, and meaningful relationships. Although pride is frequently at the root of anger, other factors also contribute. Our personalities, family upbringing, age, life experience, and spiritual maturity contribute to how we handle anger.

When Anger Becomes Dangerous

We all feel anger. We would not be human if we did not. Anger is a normal, even healthy, response in many circumstances. Anger becomes harmful and dangerous when it is persistent, repeated, and unresolved. Anger has its place and levels in each one of us. Let's think of anger at three levels.

The Levels of Anger

Misdirected Anger

If a man said he never became angry, I would ask if he was still alive. Anger, at some level, is a constant element of an emotional life. I have never met a person who did not get angry at some time. I think I am an example of a person who experiences some anger but rarely expresses it. Part of my way of handling anger results from my personality, part from my training and experience over the years, and part from the requirements of my job.

I, like many men, generally subdue my anger rather than express it. The problem is that it can be a subduing of many emotions, not just anger.

My family rarely sees me angry. In fact, that has been a hindrance to some of them. They have told me that I am too emotionally level. They want me to become upset and angry on their behalf, for example, when a boyfriend mistreats them or they are treated unjustly. But I am so much a "balancer" and "soother of conflict" that I tend to plead the other person's case.

In the few times my anger has bubbled over, it actually frightened or intimidated them. I was never explosive, but intense and obvious. As a result I found I had to learn how I could handle my anger. I, like many men, generally subdue my anger rather than express it. The problem is that it can be a subduing of many emotions, not just anger.

Most of us know when our anger is appropriate and within biblical and proper bounds. Anger toward injustice, evil in our community, or sin in our own lives is where it is appropriate. Anger in these cases can sharpen our thinking and resolve. It can galvanize us into action. It can thrust us into the role of protector and defender.

That is not to say that anger is never a problem for a person like me. When I am angry at not getting my way, at others for not performing up to my expectation, at my wife when we are in conflict, or at my children when they disobey — then I cross that line into sin. I may not express the anger inappropriately, but I know it is still there.

Usually when a person expresses his anger in an inappropriate or hurtful way, he feels almost immediate remorse and regret. That is when an apology is in order and is normally given. There are many times when I have had to ask for forgiveness from my family and others.

The Gray Middle Road of Anger

Even though some men know that all anger is not sin, they still find themselves getting angry far too often and expressing it emotionally more than they should. They do not fit the "angry man" profile, but still sense their anger crossing that unhealthy boundary for them.

The cool silence with your wife certainly tells you that something is wrong. You would never hit or hurt anyone physically, but you still sense a crossed boundary of normal irritation to anger that hurts yourself and others.

What is the evidence that you are walking this middle road of anger? The first evidence is that you see it in yourself. Your conscience quickly registers the emotions of irritation turning to anger. You always have a chance to stop its progress. When you do not stop it, it either gets bottled up inside or fleshes out in harsh words and actions. When it is consistently held inside, it often results in ulcers, depression, and discouragement. When it expresses itself naturally, it causes tension, conflict, and broken relationships.

A comment from your child, "Daddy, why are you mad at me?" is a sad reminder that you slipped over the line. The cool silence with your wife certainly tells you that something is wrong. You would never hit or hurt anyone physically, but you still sense a crossed boundary of normal irritation to anger that hurts yourself and others. I have crossed this boundary at times myself—usually within the confines of my family. I did not like having to ask forgiveness of my wife or children.

Another situation we find ourselves in is when people at work whisper, "Don't talk to Frank today. He got up on the wrong side of the bed!" You may not hear them say it, but you know you are "grumpy" and you sense people staying away. Those are times when we don't know exactly what is best—to hide it or let it show. When we hide our irritation and anger, there is a good chance we can get to the root. So often, however, it just eats at us with no resolutions.

Explosive Anger

A few men have what I call "Explosive Anger." It resides inside, often surfacing to harm others emotionally and, at times, physically.

Greg knew he had a problem with anger. It showed in his eyes, his posture, and his tone of voice. His father was abusive, having beaten him regularly. His wife tried to pacify and balance his extremes through the years. He had a son who was out of control, acting just as he did. Uncontrollable and explosive anger. Violent behavior. Verbal battles.

Greg was on the edge of physically abusing his wife. She ran. He pled and promised, as he had many times before, that he would change. He was a believer with a desire to walk with God. But an inner fire of anger controlled him. He finally became desperate enough to seek help.

He gave little indication in public of his volatile nature. Most people saw a capable, intense, hard working, and competitive man.

So it is for some of us. The anger resides deep within us. Most of the time we control the anger. Occasionally it explodes within the family or during high stress situations. Between explosions we feel it simmering inwardly.

This explosive anger is destructive to ourselves, our children, our marriages, and our relationships. Some men feel helpless, knowing it is wrong, but not able to control it. So often, our family background or peer environment as a young person stimulates and ignites this anger. But it is possible to get victory over it.

Each of these three levels of anger have a measure of sin. Clearly, explosive anger is the worst. But the others are also issues of character that God wants to change in us.

The Bible's View of Anger

Three Scriptures capture the biblical view of anger:

> Do not be quickly provoked in your spirit, for anger resides in the lap of fools. (Ecclesiastes 7:9)

> A fool gives full vent to his anger, but a wise man keeps himself under control. (Proverbs 29:11)

> An angry man stirs up dissension, and a hot-tempered one commits many sins. (Proverbs 29:22)

These are blunt statements. An angry man is a fool. A wise man controls anger. Anger causes conflict. Anger leads to sin—many sins.

The first murder in the Bible resulted from anger. Cain was angry against God, very angry. God confronted him on his anger, identifying it as the attempt of Satan to destroy him. Cain carried out his anger by murdering his brother, Abel (Genesis 4).

Famous men of the Bible destroyed their lives by anger. Moses, the man who knew God face-to-face, struck the rock to get water for the people when God instructed him to speak to it. In anger and frustration with the people he said, "Listen, you rebels, must we bring you water out of this rock?" Then, "Moses raised his arm and struck the rock twice with his staff. Water gushed out. But the LORD said to Moses and Aaron, 'Because you did not trust in me enough to honor me as holy in the sight of the Israelites, you will not bring this community into the land I give them'" (Numbers 20:10-12).

Famous men of the Bible destroyed their lives by anger

Moses acted in anger and lost his dream. Note that his anger was not violent. He was not an angry man. Yet at a moment of crisis he yielded to it.

Samson, the strong man who was a judge of Israel, lived a life of disastrous anger and lust. It finally killed him.

In most cases, anger precedes sin. Anger is listed as "fits of rage" along with sexual immorality, impurity, debauchery, idolatry, and witchcraft in Galatians 5:19,20. It poisons our physical and spiritual life as well as our relationships. We cannot excuse anger by blaming personality or background.

What results when we do not deal with anger in our lives? When anger boils out in verbal ways or by outward attributes of sullenness, irritability, or other nonverbal signals easily recognized by family and friends it:

- causes tensions
- engenders conflict
- hurts those closest to us
- leaves us with guilt and regret
- breaks friendships
- ruins work relationships
- intimidates and frightens our children

If you have explosive anger you recognize these results all too well. It is especially damaging in the family. To see children cower in our presence should be enough to cause us to change. A little boy or girl should never have to question, "Why is Daddy mad at me?" Whether or not our anger is resolved internally, it devastates those around us.

Anger turned inward:

- gives us ulcers
- makes us physically ill
- derails spiritual growth
- affects our entire outlook on life
- robs us of joy

So what do we do with anger? It is damaging to express it or internalize it, yet it is still such a prominent part of many men's lives.

Several steps can be taken to effect permanent change in any pattern of anger you may see in yourself.

1. Admit to yourself that you have a problem with anger. Admit that it is sin. Recognize it as an offense against God (Ephesians 4:31). Confess it to God asking for His forgiveness.
2. Share the problem with a close friend and ask him to hold you accountable for change. This will provide a place where you can talk through some of your feelings on your anger.
3. Ask your wife, children, or others close to you for forgiveness. This is not an easy step. Tell them you want to change and ask for both their patience and help.
4. With your close friend discuss and write out what you perceive causes your anger. Possibilities are basic personality, habit patterns, not getting your way, pride, a shallow walk with God, not wanting to admit you are wrong, fear of failure, etcetera. Likely, you will find one or two primary sources.
5. Ask God to change you. Make some specific commitments for which you will be held accountable.

    In extreme cases, you may need the help of a biblically oriented counselor.

    You will be amazed at the change you will sense in your life and relationships.

I assure you that there is real hope, and discouraging as anger is, God gives the incredible replacement of love, joy, peace, longsuffering, temperance, gentleness, goodness, faith and meekness (Galatians 5:22-23, KJV). These are promised fruits of the Spirit. I have seen men change radically—both externally and internally.

Be kind and compassionate to one another, forgiving each other, just as in Christ God forgave you (Ephesians 4:32).

QUESTIONS FOR THOUGHT AND DISCUSSION

1. What is it like to be around an angry person?

2. What is the difference between expressing legitimate frustration and sinful episodes of anger?

3. Why is it a foolish thing to give full vent to one's anger?

4. What is the relationship between anger and sin? Has uncontrolled anger spilled over into other areas of your life, perhaps creating more sin? Have you ever sinned when you were angry, feeling your anger gave you the right to do so?

5. What happens when we fail to recognize and deal with anger in our lives?

6. Are there specific situations that routinely make you angry?

7. How can you begin to discover the root causes of anger when it's out of control?

8. How do you relate to God when you are angry? Are you able to do so?

9. What do you do when you're angry at God? Can we express anger toward God without it being sin? Is it ever okay to express anger toward God?

SCRIPTURAL INSIGHTS:

1. Read Proverbs 29, Ecclesiastes 7:9, and James 3. What do you learn about anger and its sources? What can you do to deal with anger?

CHAPTER THIRTEEN

WHEN PRIDE BECOMES SIN

An egotist is not a man who thinks
too much of himself. He is a man
who thinks too little of other people.
OSCAR WILDE

EARLY in my Air Force career, I was stationed at Patrick Air Force Base, Florida, the headquarters for the Atlantic Missile Range and the Air Force Missile Test Center at Cape Canaveral. Mary and I were heavily involved in the Base chapel program. The pianist at the chapel was not very skilled. When the opportunity came for Mary to play for the services the first time, she recounted her feelings.

"I had been critical of the skill of the person who had been playing the piano. When my turn came, I thought, 'Wait until they hear how it really should be done.' The music that day went well and I was feeling smug. Then in the silence during the pastoral prayer, the hymnbook fell from the music rack onto the piano keys, loudly disturbing the silence of the moment, and shattering my pride. On the way home Jerry laughed; I cried all the way, embarrassed and humiliated. Yet it is one of the best lessons that could have happened to get at my pride."

A Life-Changing Experience

We have to get rid of the idea that we understand ourselves. That is always the last bit of pride to go. The only One who understands us is God. The greatest curse in our spiritual life is pride. If we have ever had a glimpse of what we are like in the sight of God, we will never say, "Oh, I'm so unworthy." We will understand that this goes without saying.

Even though being a mission controller at Cape Canaveral was a highlight of my life as well as life-changing in terms of my professional direction, I cannot help but think how I got there.

When I entered the Air Force I embarked on a year of pilot training. I was rather blasé about it all. I did reasonably well and was coasting along near the end of my year in the final phase of jet training in the T-33. In my formation check ride I made an error on take-off that allowed the nose wheel to become "cocked" on the power run-up at the end of the runway. This caused me to fall behind the lead aircraft about fifty yards as I lifted off. I got caught in the lead plane's jet wash and the plane suddenly banked in a dangerous way. I was shaken!

The rest of the flight was a disaster. I failed miserably. On a recheck two days later I flew reasonably well, but the check pilot simply said, "You can fly it, but not well enough to fly four-ship formation." Then he gave me a failing grade and I was out! No recourse.

Up to this point in my life I had not failed in any significant way. Life had been one success after another. My pride was wounded. After all, why be in the Air Force if I could not fly? So I asked God, and the

Air Force, to give me an engineering assignment anywhere. I planned to serve my mandatory three years and get out. God intervened and through no effort on my part, put me in the midst of the new space program. I could not have planned it better. But first God had to wound my pride. I wish I could say it was broken, but it was not. There was much to come in my life that would cause me to deal with my prideful spirit.

The Motives of the Heart

Writing a chapter on pride is very difficult. I feel hypocritical since I see so many issues of pride in my life. I have chosen to use primarily personal illustrations (or Mary's, with her permission). I feel it is virtually impossible to discern if another person is prideful. Pride is more a motive of the heart than it is of action. One man may appear prideful but does not have prideful motives. Another man may appear humble yet be driven by intense pride. I find it difficult to know exactly when I am being motivated by pride.

Paul correctly describes this dilemma:

> I care very little if I am judged by you or by any human court; indeed, I do not even judge myself. My conscience is clear, but that does not make me innocent. It is the Lord who judges me. Therefore judge nothing before the appointed time; wait till the Lord comes. He will bring to light what is hidden in darkness and will excuse the motives of men's hearts. (1 Corinthians 4:4-5)

Only God really knows our motives fully.

Oswald Chambers writes:

> We have to get rid of the idea that we understand ourselves. That is always the last bit of pride to go. The only One who understands us is God. The greatest curse in our spiritual life is pride. If we have ever had a glimpse of what we are like in the sight of God, we will never say, "Oh, I'm so unworthy."

We will understand that this goes without saying. Whenever there is any element of pride or conceit remaining, Jesus can't teach us anything. He will allow us to experience heartbreak or the disappointment we feel when our intellectual pride is wounded.[1]

It seems that heartbreak and disappointment are primary means God uses to break the bonds of pride in our lives. I wonder why it is so hard? Why can't we just decide to be humble? The root is the sinful nature that still tries to control us.

God's View of Pride

God does not mince words in His view of pride. "Whoever has haughty eyes and a proud heart, him will I not endure" (Psalm 101:5). "I hate pride and arrogance, evil behavior and perverse speech" (Proverbs 8:13). The message is simple. God will not tolerate pride. He will do whatever He must to dig it out at the roots.

Every man wants to be a success and to achieve and accomplish. That is normal and right. God made us that way. The problem arises when we take the credit.

Pride is the most subtle of all the dangers. No one denies its presence. But most of us do not recognize its power over us nor the constancy of the battle with it. We recognize it, then ignore it. We become used to its presence and excuse its badness as a friend to be tolerated. We rebuke it and it recedes temporarily, only to appear again in a different suit of clothes. We disdain its hold on us, yet feel insecure and undressed without it. Such is pride—slippery and elusive, deadly and destructive.

In spiritual moments you might say, "How could anyone tolerate sinful pride?" as though there were any other kind. It comes in such attractive and compelling forms. Pride of person, success, possession, and position.

Pride of person portends to take credit for who we are. Our intellect, race, abilities, appearance, and upbringing each demand a place in our pride. Yet we had, or have, no control over any of them. "What do you have that you did not receive?" (1 Corinthians 4:7) is drowned out by "Look at me? Aren't I something?" All that we have in our person is from God, by His grace. We did nothing to earn it.

But we can do much to spoil it. We are commanded to be thankful for our heritage and the sovereign creation of our person. We take pride and care in this creation. We respect and value it in ourselves and others. God deeply values us as His creation. But we cannot take credit for it. Pride has no just foundation here.

Every man wants to be a success and to achieve and accomplish. That is normal and right. God made us that way. The problem arises when we take the credit.

The King's Pride

Babylon, in the country of Iraq, fifty-five miles south of modern Baghdad, was once one of the greatest cities in the world. In it were the Hanging Gardens of Babylon, one of the seven wonders of the ancient world. Babylon was an impressive triple-walled city of eleven miles circumference. It stood on the bank of the Euphrates River, possibly the site of the famed ziggurat—the tower of Babel. The city's ruins still stand as a silent testimony to past splendor. With a population of 100,000 and over 1100 temples, it was the greatest city of its time (6th and 7th centuries B.C.).

Nebuchadnezzar II reigned as king of the Chaldean empire from 605 to 562 B.C. During his father's reign, he was a brilliant military strategist, leading the historic victory over the Egyptians at Carchemish in 605 B.C.

The victory established Babylonian authority over all western Asia, thus ranking it as one of the most decisive battles of all time. One of Nebuchadnezzar's key advisors was the Jewish captive, Daniel. Nebuchadnezzar built the hanging gardens and most of the city. It was a city of incredible beauty and splendor. He was a great and brilliant king.

In Daniel 4, Nebuchadnezzar had a strange dream which only Daniel was able to interpret. Daniel was terrified at the dream since it predicted disaster for the king.

> You have become great and strong; your greatness has grown until it reaches the sky, and your dominion extends to distant parts of the earth. . . . This is the decree the Most High has issued against my lord the king: You will be driven away from people and will live with the wild animals; you will eat grass like cattle and be drenched with the dew of heaven. (Daniel 4:22,25)

To avoid this disaster, Daniel counseled, "Therefore, O king, be pleased to accept my advice: Renounce your sins by doing what is right, and your wickedness by being kind to the oppressed. It may be that then your prosperity will continue" (Daniel 4:27).

Twelve months later, Nebuchadnezzar stood on the roof of his palace in Babylon looking over the great city.

> "Is not this the great Babylon which I have built as the royal residence, by my mighty power and for the glory of my majesty?" The words were still on his lips when a voice came from heaven, "This is what is decreed for you, King Nebuchadnezzar: Your royal authority has been taken from you. You will be driven away from people and will live with the wild animals; you will eat grass like cattle. Seven times will pass by for you until you acknowledge that the Most High is sovereign over the kingdoms of men and gives them to anyone he wishes." (Daniel 4:37)

That is exactly what happened.

Later his son (or possibly grandson) Belshazzar became king. This time Daniel, now an old man, was called to interpret handwriting that appeared on the wall during a drunken feast. Daniel told him of Nebuchadnezzar, "But when his heart became arrogant and hardened with pride, he was deposed from his royal throne and stripped of his glory" (Daniel 5:20).

Honoring God in Our Success

The message is clear. God will not tolerate arrogance or pride over our success or achievements. We may receive honor, but we must give the honor to God. That is easy to say, but not so easy to do in our hearts. Somehow we still think that we achieved it on our own. We have simply been using the gifts God gave us to do what He wanted.

Whether in business, education, craftsmanship, speaking, or earning money, any success is from God. Any success can be reversed in a moment, so we dare not become proud. "A man's pride brings him low" (Proverbs 29:23).

Possessions and wealth can easily make a person proud. We see it about us daily. Wealth is relative. Wealthy compared to whom? Each of us is more wealthy or has more possessions than someone else. It is all a matter of perspective. It seems that the amount matters little.

One man has an extra pickup truck and a small fishing boat in addition to his house and he feels like he has a lot. Another man has three cars, a house on the lake, a large home, and always strives to get more. The important principle is in how we view our possessions, not how much we have.

The Scriptures are filled with teaching and warning on money and possessions. "Whoever trusts in his riches will fall, but the righteous will thrive like a green leaf" (Proverbs 11:28). "Watch out! Be on your guard against all kinds of greed; a man's life does not consist in the abundance of his possessions" (Luke 12:15).

Pride in possessions can be a subtle trap. We get so used to having nice things—a good home, or an excess of money—that we forget what it was like not to have them and we grow to expect them as a right.

The worst kind of pride comes when we look down on others who do not have much. I have noticed how people avoid men who are unemployed. Some jobless men have told me it is as if they had become a leper.

Wealth and possessions are so temporary that it is amazing that we depend so much on them. "Do not wear yourself out to get rich; have the wisdom to show restraint. Cast but a glance at riches, and they are gone, for they will surely sprout wings and fly off to the sky like an eagle" (Proverbs 23:4-5).

Biblical Instruction on Wealth

The most basic instruction on wealth and possessions is in the New Testament outline of the attitude God desires. "Keep your lives free from the love of money and be content with what you have, because God has said, "Never will I leave you; never will I forsake you!"" (Hebrews 13:5).

> For we brought nothing into the world, and we can take nothing out of it. But if we have food and clothing, we will be content with that. People who want to get rich fall into temptation and a trap and into many foolish and harmful desires that plunge men into ruin and destruction. For the love of money is a root of all kinds of evil. Some people, eager for money, have wandered from the faith and pierced themselves with many griefs. . . . Command those who are rich in this present world not to be arrogant nor to put their hope in wealth, which is so uncertain, but to put their hope in God, who richly provides us with everything for our enjoyment. Command them to do good, to be rich in good deeds, and to be generous and willing to share. In this way they will lay up treasures for themselves as a firm foundation for the coming age, so that they may take hold of the life that is truly life. (1 Timothy 6:7-10, 17-19)

Life that is truly life. That is what we all want. But it does not come as a result of any wealth. We must resist any pride that wells up in us regarding our possessions, for they are temporary. Yet we are taught that we can enjoy them freely as from God.

Pride of Position

Finally, consider pride of position. I discussed much of this in chapter four on loss of position. Pride of position in your work, your society, your neighborhood, or your church can quietly invade the mind. "Do they know who I am? If they knew, they would treat me better."

I am sad to say that this comes up in my own life far more frequently than I wish. Every time I think of using the title "doctor" or "general" I am filled with a question of pride. I silently want people to know.

Any position is temporary. All positions are from God, to be used for His glory.

> *Pride is the only disease known to man that makes everyone rich except the one who has it.*
>
> BUDDY ROBINSON

The Consequences of Pride
When I allow pride a place in my life, what results can I expect?

- *It will cause us to fall.* "Pride goes before destruction, a haughty spirit before a fall" (Proverbs 16:18).
- *It puts us in danger of God's anger.* "The Lord detests all the proud of heart. Be sure of this: they will not go unpunished" (Proverbs 16:5).
- *It brings disgrace.* "When pride comes, then comes disgrace, but with humility comes wisdom" (Proverbs 11:2).
- *It engenders conflict.* "Pride only breeds quarrels" (Proverbs 13:10).

The antithesis of pride is humility. It is the character trait that God honors. "All of you, clothe yourselves with humility toward one another" (1 Peter 5:5). Then, as the passage goes on to state, God will exalt or promote us in His good timing.

> *How is humility built? Usually through suffering.*

How is humility built? Usually through suffering. When our son was murdered, I found that so much of what I had been prideful about didn't matter at all. My outlook on what was important changed dramatically. But even in that terrible time, I saw pride rearing its ugly head.

Larry Crabb, in his book *Finding God*, reflects this idea.

> Within days of my brother's death, I spoke at his memorial
> service. As I prepared my few comments on behalf of our family,
> I prayed that God would use my stumbling tongue in this diffi-
> cult situation to encourage others to trust in the goodness of God
> no matter what might happen in their lives. I wanted to give.
> At one point during my talk, I noticed that a phrase I had
> just used was especially rich. As any experienced public
> speaker might do, I paused to let that phrase sink in. During
> that three-second pause, I heard these words run through my
> mind, "I'm doing a pretty good job. That was a good pause."
> Immediately, I felt slapped in the face by the realization that
> at that moment I cared more about how I was performing
> than about how meaningfully I was ministering.
> That night I wept bitterly. I grieve that even at my
> brother's funeral I couldn't escape the wretched power
> of pride.[2]

So we struggle to remove that root of pride that so deeply offends
God and causes us to sin.

> Whoever loves money never has
>   money enough;
> Whoever loves wealth is never
>   satisfied with his income.
> This too is meaningless.
> (Ecclesiastes 5:10)

The one constant of all mankind is pride. Whether subtle and hidden or blatant and obvious, it permeates too much of our lives. Then
so much of our spiritual growth is tied to the replacing of pride by
Christlike humility. We desperately need the instruction of 1 Peter
5:6, "Humble yourselves, therefore, under God's mighty hand, that
he may lift you up in due time."

Is there any antidote for these dangers of sin—sexual temptation,
anger, conflict, and pride? We now turn to such a possibility.

QUESTIONS FOR THOUGHT AND DISCUSSION

1. What are some evidences of pride? When you see them, how do you feel?

2. What's the difference between "sinful pride" and being proud of your accomplishments or those of your children and grand-children?

3. How do you identify pride in yourself? Is it acceptable if it doesn't show externally? Why or why not?

4. What are some events in your life that have helped deal with the issue of pride?

SCRIPTURAL INSIGHTS:

1. Read 1 Peter 5:5-6, Philippians 2:5-13, and Proverbs 6:16-19. What do these passages teach you about pride and humility? How is Christ our example?

CHAPTER FOURTEEN

THE ANTIDOTE FOR SIN

WHEN Mary's cancer was discovered in 1994 she had back-to-back radiation therapy appointments with a dear friend and Navigator staff wife, Carolyn North. Two years later Carolyn has died and Mary is cancer free, to the best of our knowledge. We reflected that Mary could also have been taken in death. From a spiritual perspective, God is sovereign. From a human perspective, several issues clearly emerge.

Anyone who has had cancer knows the critical factors intimately. Early detection. Immediate action. Attempt at complete removal and eradication. Preventative treatment for recurrence.

Mary's cancer was completely removed surgically with preventative treatment to follow. Carolyn's could not be completely erased.

Sin is a cancer of the soul. It intrudes and destroys. It resists detection and treatment. It is persistent and devious.

Principles for the Detection of the Cancer of Sin

If only the antidote for sin were as simple as the detection and removal of cancer. Yet the principles are similar.

Early Detection

Procrastination is a terrible habit. It keeps us in bondage to all of the undone tasks of our lives. Procrastination of certain cancer detecting tests often costs lives. We all know that Pap tests and breast exams for women, and prostate checks for men are a must.

Procrastination regarding sin is just as disastrous. The longer we allow the poison to remain in our lives, the more damage will be done. Ask God to reveal specific areas of sin to you. Look for it. Detect it early, before it gets a lifelong grip on you. "Search me, O God, and know my heart; test me and know my anxious thoughts. See if there is any offensive way in me, and lead me in the way everlasting" (Psalm 139:23-24).

When you ask God to do this for you, He will. Once you have seen and admitted to yourself that you have sinned, you can get an antidote working.

David went through this process regarding his adultery with Bathsheba in Psalm 51. "For I know my transgressions, and my sin is always before me." David was very conscious of his need.

Immediate Action

"Cleanse me with hyssop, and I will be clean; wash me, and I will be whiter than snow. Let me hear joy and gladness; let the bones you have crushed rejoice. . . . Create in me a pure heart, O God, and renew a steadfast spirit within me. . . . Restore to me the joy of your salvation and grant me a willing spirit, to sustain me" (Psalm 51:3,7,8,10,12).

David knew he must take action. He could not delay. Yet, he appears to have delayed long enough to suffer emotionally before he confessed. The longer we wait, the more difficult it becomes to take corrective action. Like David, we feel unclean, we lack joy and we feel crushed. I think, though, that when David finally realized what he had done, he took action. It actually was his friend Nathan who confronted him with his sin. Later we will discuss the importance of accountability.

Confession

What first action is required regarding sin? It is *confession*.

Confession is the open admission to God of our sin. "If we confess our sins, He is faithful and just and will forgive us our sins and purify us from all unrighteousness" (1 John 1:9).

To confess means to admit our guilt, assent to God's sovereign standards, and agree with God that our actions are unacceptable (repentance—turning from our sin). This confession results in forgiveness, which restores our fellowship with God. It is not gaining salvation. Our salvation is assured if we have received Christ as Savior. We also do not confess with the inner thought that we can sin in the same way again. We need the mindset of stopping that sinful habit, action, or thought.

> *Confession is not trivial or just a quick naming of the sin. It is a deep admission of an offense to God.*

Confession is not trivial or just a quick naming of the sin. It is a deep admission of an offense to God. Nor is it an "Oh, I've been caught, so I might as well admit it" type of confession. Rather, it is the sense that David had in saying, "Against you, you only, have I sinned and done what is evil in your sight" (Psalm 51:4). A deep spirit of contrition accompanies confession. There is real remorse over our sin.

What about Uriah and Bathsheba? Did David sin against them? Yes, but his confession is primarily to God. He would live with and pay for his sin the rest of his human life. And so may we. Did he ask forgiveness of Bathsheba? We do not know from Scripture, but I assume he did.

Sin damages us and others deeply and often permanently. Confession may also need to be offered to other people depending on the nature of the sin. This involves *restoration* and *reconciliation*. But one step precedes this.

Complete Removal

Just as cancer must be completely removed to render it ineffective, so sin must be completely removed. With confession sin is immediately removed in terms of our relationship with God. Sin is forgiven and we are cleansed. He removed the eternal penalty when we first became a believer. The door for fellowship with God is opened again.

However, recurrence of this sin is not precluded. Some preventative measures need to be taken. It is not at all uncommon for sin to persist and discourage us with its reappearance. Thus, confession needs to be accompanied by repentance.

Repentance

Repentance is a conscious attitude of regret, a changing of the mind or a turning from sin to God. This involves a reorientation to God.

In the Greek, *metanoia* (repentance) is the noun form of the verb *metaneo* (repent). The noun *repentance* indicates a reversal or turning around. The verb implies thinking differently. Repentance is active. "Produce fruit in keeping with repentance" (Luke 3:8).

Acts 3:19 shows the sequence and results. "Repent then, and turn to God, so that your sins may be wiped out, that times of refreshing may come from the Lord." Acts 26:20 ties this to our actions following repentance: "prove their repentance by their deeds."

We do not repent with our fingers crossed, indicating that we don't really mean it. Real change is required. Change demands effort. In 1 John 1:9 confession implies, even demands, repentance. They go hand in hand.

Does this mean that you will never commit this sin again? Not necessarily. But the intent of your heart must be that you will not. You now need the power of the Holy Spirit to keep your pledge of repentance.

A Christian leader told of his ten-year bondage to the sin of lust, which included a regular diet of pornography. During this time, he was conducting Christian conferences and seminars across the country. The agony of his inner conflict finally became unbearable. To his horror he realized one day that such pleasures as a breathtaking sunset or the soft spray of an ocean breeze no longer excited him. His obsession with lust had dulled his appreciation of life's finest enjoyments and prevented the joy of fellowshipping with Jesus. Outwardly he had been faithful to his wife, not having engaged in adultery. Yet he had sinned against her, and their relationship had suffered. When he turned anew to God, he realized that a necessary step in the breaking of his lustful pattern was a long talk with his mate. The whole experience was painful and awkward, but the repentance was genuine. She forgave him, and new love soon returned to their marriage.

> *The agony of his inner conflict finally became unbearable. To his horror he realized one day that such pleasures as a breathtaking sunset or the soft spray of an ocean breeze no longer excited him.*

C. S. Lewis said that ". . . a Christian is not a man who never goes wrong, but a man who is enabled to repent and pick himself up and begin over again after each stumble—because the Christ-life is inside him, repairing him all the time . . . ."[1]

Repentance requires action. Words simply prayed are not sufficient. Repentance involves true sorrow for sin. Paul confronted the believers in Corinth with their terrible moral and relational sin in 1 Corinthians. In his second letter he described how those believers responded: "Even if I caused you sorrow by my letter, I do not regret it. Though I did regret it—I see that my letter hurt you, but only for a little while—yet now I am happy, not because you were made sorry, but because *your sorrow led you to repentance.* For you became sorrowful as God intended. . . . Godly sorrow brings repentance that leads to salvation and leaves no regret, but worldly sorrow brings death" (2 Corinthians 7:8-10, emphasis added).

True repentance produces a deep sense of having offended a holy God, a sorrow that is God-induced. Worldly sorrow is being sorry for getting caught or having hurt someone, but lacks the dimension of deep offense to God.

The human result of confession and repentance is a tremendous feeling of being clean. It is a new lease on life. *The Message* describes it in this way:

> And now isn't it wonderful all the ways in which this distress has goaded you closer to God? You're more alive, more concerned, more sensitive, more reverent, more human, more passionate, more responsible. Looked at from any angle, you've come out of this with purity of heart. (2 Corinthians 7:11)

That is what we want—purity of heart. What greater result of cleansing is there than purity of heart and peace of mind?

Preventative Treatment—Accountability

When my children were growing up, a favorite statement after being corrected was, "Dad! Nobody's perfect!" So true. None of us can ever say with 100 percent confidence, "I'll never do that again." We are fallen men in a fallen world. It is a world of sin and temptation.

Accountability is an important part of prevention, but there is something even more basic. God has made provision for us to overcome sin. Continuing our discussion from chapter nine, we recall that God, in Christ, has paid the penalty for sin once and for all. Yet sins (plural) still invade our lives.

Two statements stand out in Romans 6. The first tells us:

> Therefore do not let sin reign in your mortal body so that you obey its evil desires. Do not offer the parts of your body to sin, as instruments of wickedness, but rather offer yourselves to God, as those who have been brought from death to life;

and offer the parts of your body to him as instruments of righteousness. (Romans 6:12-13)

This passage says that we choose not to offer ourselves to sin. We have the power to make this choice because of the second statement, a promise: "For sin shall not be your master, because you are not under law, but under grace" (Romans 6:14).

The death of our old self does not make us sinless but gives us the freedom and the power to *choose* to serve sin or to serve righteousness. Prior to salvation we had no choice. Now we do.

We choose to refuse to let sin reign over (control) us. Our human nature still responds to temptation to sin. But we choose to resist it by our will and by the power of the Holy Spirit (Galatians 5:16,24 and Romans 8:4-8). I will discuss this in more depth in chapter eighteen.

A Path for Righteous Living

Most believing men I know do want to live a life that honors God. In the Gospels, Jesus gives us a number of commands to help us walk this path of righteous living:

1. Come to me (Matthew 11:28-30). When we come to Him, He enables us. He leads us. But He gives us the option to voluntarily come.
2. Follow me (John 12:25-26). We follow Him by giving up our right to live life on our terms. A believer could be described as a follower of Christ. As we follow Him, we learn from Him. We experience His companionship and receive His guidance.
3. Seek His Kingdom and His righteousness first (Matthew 6:33). This is giving God the first priority in our lives. Seeking implies an effort to put Christ and His kingdom first in our decisions. This command is in the context of our need for material and physical things. This ought to be our daily goal.

4. Go deep with God (Luke 6:48). The familiar story of a house built on sand or rock shows that as we spend time with God daily and as we study His Word, we build foundations that will endure the incessant trials of life and the invasion of sin. Poor foundations make for weak buildings.

5. Keep alert and keep going (Matthew 26:41). Vigilance against sin is a necessity. We cannot rest on our past purity. There is no assurance of holiness like assurance of salvation. The flesh is weak. Only through the power of the Holy Spirit can we keep walking righteously.

6. Go and tell (Matthew 28:18-20). A life committed to tell people about Christ and His love will help us avoid sin. As I travel I do get tempted in many ways. When I am tempted in an airport bookstore, my commitment to share the gospel helps me resist picking up books or magazines that are not holy or healthy. I often have conversations with people in airports or airplanes. What if they saw me violating what they know should be my standards?

Human Accountability

We nurture a life pattern of preventing sin by keeping close to God. There is also a human element of accountability. One of the things that keeps me pursuing God and turning from sin is an accountability relationship with three other men.

Vigilance against sin is a necessity. We cannot rest on our past purity.

Although we had been friends for a number of years, in 1988 we decided to formalize our covenant and accountability. Our basic purpose is not simply to help one another keep from sinning, but to keep us faithful in our walk with God.

One of the men, Doug Hignell said, "Humble myself enough to be accountable to another person? Not me, a man who likes to be in control and paddle his own canoe!" That would have been my response fifteen years ago.

Doug went on to say, "But as I began to grow in my spiritual

THE ANTIDOTE FOR SIN 129

walk, and as God brought men with spiritual depth into my life, being a lone ranger became less attractive. I began to realize that to remain teachable as I got older and to end well in my Christian walk, I needed to develop one or more relationships that would require me to keep open and vulnerable."[2]

Doug, Stan, Chris, and I have made this covenant to help each other finish well. Our wives have also made this covenant with us and with each other. We have given one another full permission to invade each others' lives, to ask any questions.

> A friend loves at all times, and a brother is born for adversity.
> (Proverbs 17:17)
>
> Carry each other's burdens, and in this way you will fulfill the law of Christ. (Galatians 6:2)

This is what the four of us try to do for each other.

We desperately need each other. Unfortunately, no amount of accountability will keep a person from sin if he sets his mind on sinning. Accountability inhibits sin, it does not prevent it. The best accountability is not where men who are acquaintances get together with a list of questions. That can be helpful as a minimum inhibitor.

Accountability inhibits sin, it does not prevent it.

The best accountability is with very close friends who know each other so well that they "sense" when something is going astray, and will say so. If, however, you do not open up your life, no one will invade it, even in a crisis. The one downside to accountability in a close friendship is that a close friend can assume too much. He may fear losing your friendship if he becomes suspicious and aggressively ask questions. We want to think the best of people. It is best to have accountability in a group setting with two or more close friends.

The prophet Nathan was King David's friend. Knowing the power of ancient middle eastern kings, he risked not only his friendship, but his life, to confront David about his sin with Bathsheba (2 Samuel 12:1-14).

Accountability does not necessarily need to be two way. If you need it, seek it out. Pat Morely in his excellent book, *The Man in the Mirror*, defines accountability: To be regularly *answerable* for each of the *key areas* of our lives to *qualified* people (emphasis added).[3]

He also includes what he calls the "iceberg" illustrations. On the surface are casual conversations on sports, politics, weather, etc. Below the surface lurk the real issues: secret thought life, ambitions, motives, marriage issues, moral and ethical behavior, relationship with God and others, use of time and money, the past, and much more.[4]

No one goes below the surface immediately. But the goal is to reveal what is below the surface of your life. "Make this your common practice: Confess your sins to each other and pray for each other so that you can live together whole and healed" (James 5:16, MSG).

Without accountability, we are very much alone. Then sin will isolate us even more:

> Two are better than one, because they have a good return for their work. If one falls down, his friend can help him up. But pity the man who falls and has no one to help him up! . . . Though one may be overpowered, two can defend themselves. A cord of three strands is not quickly broken. (Ecclesiastes 4:9,10,12)

The letter I wrote in chapter ten gives a few ideas on what to ask in an accountability setting. Morely also gives an excellent accountability checkup list.[5]

Restoration, Reconciliation, and Restitution

These three "R's" often must accompany confession of sin for full healing to occur. Consider the definition of each:

Restoration
Restoration means bringing back to original or former condition. If you have sinned against a friend, the friendship needs restoration. When God forgives us we are restored to fellowship with Him.

When Jesus healed a withered hand or a blind eye, the Bible says he restored them. In Galatians 6:1, the apostle Paul explains that when a person sins, we are to restore him gently.

Reconciliation

Reconciliation means to bring about harmony, agreement, or a settlement, to make peace when parties have been at variance with each other.

We are reconciled to God by the blood of Jesus Christ. In terms of relationships with others, when there are conflicts and offenses we are to be reconciled or brought into harmony before we can worship. "Therefore, if you are offering your gift at the altar and there remember that your brother has something against you, leave your gift there in front of the altar. First go and be reconciled to your brother; then come and offer your gift" (Matthew 5:23-24).

Restitution

Restitution is compensation for a wrong done, repayment of a debt, or redress for harm done. Returning what has wrongfully been taken.

Throughout the Bible restitution is promoted. A sign of righteousness and justice is to pay back what is taken, stolen, lost, or damaged. When Zacchaeus encountered Jesus in Luke 19:1-10, his response was, "If I have cheated anybody out of anything, I will pay back four times the amount."

After sinning, we have an obligation to make things right with people against whom we have sinned. Even though we cannot force anyone to respond favorably to our attempts at restoration and reconciliation, we are obligated to try. "If it is possible, as far as it depends on you, live at peace with everyone" (Romans 12:18).

Some business agreements may need healing if one party did not live up to agreed obligations. If there is any question in your mind, make it right.

Restoration is something that we can do from our side only. For instance, if you are divorced you may need to review your obligation to your former wife and children.

Restoration and reconciliation are similar and often go hand in hand. However, one can restore a relationship, but still not reconcile an issue. We can agree to disagree. That often happens in marriage.

A Christian wife had a brief affair and her youngest child was the result of that illicit relationship. She concealed it from her husband, and her guilt began to drive her crazy. Finally, unable to face her husband each day, she asked him to move out of the house.

When the woman came for counseling, she was very distraught. When told that she needed to confess her sin to God and to her husband, she hesitated but soon was on her knees before the Lord.

A little later, she confessed to her husband, who was also a Christian. As she started to ask for his forgiveness, he took her in his arms and said, "I forgive you. And I love our little boy just as much as if he came from me." Today that family is living for the Lord. This would not have been the case if she had refused to humble herself, repent, and confess her sin.

> *As she started to ask for his forgiveness, he took her in his arms and said, "I forgive you. And I love our little boy just as much as if he came from me." Today that family is living for the Lord. This would not have been the case if she had refused to humble herself, repent, and confess her sin.*

Healing

If we have cancer, we want to be healed. That is the goal. We go through all the steps of identification, action, removal, treatment, and prevention to be healed, to be free of cancer. Of course, as many of us can testify from personal experience, cancer is not always eradicated. What all sinners desire is to be healed, to be free from the burden of sins that have bound us. We know God forgives, but does He heal?

Healing comes from God. It is a result of obedience. Forgiveness is instantaneous, but healing is a process. Even when we confess and repent, our emotions do not immediately catch up, particularly if our sin requires that we tell others or make attempts at reconciliation. One of the main ingredients for healing is time. "Come, let us return to the LORD. He has torn us to pieces but he will heal us; he has injured us but he will bind up our wounds. After two days he will revive us; on the third day he will restore us, that we may live in his presence. Let us acknowledge the LORD; let us press on to acknowledge him. As surely as the sun rises, he will appear; he will come to us like the winter rains, like the spring rains that water the earth (Hosea 6:1-3). *We personally need time, but also others need time for healing as our sin has impacted them.* Then we follow through with repentance, restoration, reconciliation, and restitution, allowing God and His Spirit to minister to us.

> *As surely as the sun rises, he will appear; he will come to us like the winter rains, like the spring rains that water the earth.*

"He heals the broken hearted and binds up their wounds" (Psalm 147:3). God is the healer. This promise of healing is to the brokenhearted. Sin breaks God's heart and should break ours when we sin. This is reflected in David's Psalm of Confession, "The sacrifices of God are a broken spirit; a broken and contrite heart, O God, you will not despise." (Psalm 51:17)

The context of this statement is David's desire to offer a sacrifice to atone for his sin. It is not what God wanted. God wanted a broken spirit. David's desire was to be restored to the joy of God's salvation, to be healed and at peace. That needs to be our desire, too. Pray for a broken heart over sin.

God has an antidote for each of our sins. But, like antidotes in the physical world, they are worthless and ineffective until taken and applied. A physician prescribes the medicine. We buy it and set it on our bedroom dresser. But until it is taken, it has no healing effect. So we act in humility and in obedience to the One who died so we could live—really live, not just stumble through life without joy and with persistent guilt. He wants us to experience the peace that surpasses all human understanding.

QUESTIONS FOR THOUGHT AND DISCUSSION

1. How are cancer and sin alike?

2. What happens when immediate action is not taken regarding our sin?

3. What is confession? How public should it be?

4. What is the difference between confession and repentance? Can there be one without the other?

5. What does accountability look like? Does it always work?

6. Discuss your own accountability structure.

7. Why does healing often take a long time? How complete will healing be?

SCRIPTURAL INSIGHTS:

1. Read the account of David's sin in 2 Samuel 11–12 and his confession in Psalm 51. What lessons can you learn from David? What were the consequences of his sin? How could he still be called *a man after God's own heart*?

THE DANGER
OF FREEZING

CHAPTER FIFTEEN

THE DANGER OF FREEZING

The tragedy of life is not that we die,
but rather what dies inside a man
while he still lives.
ALBERT SCHWEITZER

CHANGE is the byword of the '90s. Politicians, preachers, and corporate executives consistently present us with word pictures of change. The debate of whether or not to change comes in two themes. The first voice decries the change, calling for a return to life in the past. A second voice promotes change with dire warnings of disaster if we do not embrace it.

I could easily list the revolutionary changes taking place in computers, communication, jobs, or science, but change happens so rapidly the list would be immediately obsolete. We reel, not only from the changes, but also from the rate of change. We wish life would slow down so we could catch our breath.

Do you remember some of the relics of your past that have become obsolete? When I studied engineering, the slide rule was the key tool of my trade. Now slide rules are museum pieces.

As they grow older, men finally come to a place where they refuse to keep changing. There is comfort in the old and familiar. The old computer will do just fine and who wants to mess with a compact disc? My cassettes are good enough. These patterns of thinking are especially noticeable in the elderly, but this thinking also permeates the mind of every person who is mentally and emotionally overloaded with change.

What does matter is whether a man's thinking, perspectives, and actions have also frozen at some point in his past. A mental and emotional hardening is disastrous.

Have you seen the classic '50s man? Crew cut and leisure suits.

Or the '60s man? Long hair, pony tail and sideburns, and a hippie demeanor.

How about the '80s Yuppie? Button down shirt, Rolex watch, BMW.

You can draw your own picture of people you know who seem to have frozen in time. They set and harden like concrete, unable to change.

You might say, "What's wrong with that? Being an up-to-date fashion plate is not of high value." That is true. What does matter is whether a man's thinking, perspectives, and actions have also frozen at some point in his past. A mental and emotional hardening is disastrous.

Our world is changing rapidly in so many ways. For the sake of the gospel and for the sake of our well-being and personal growth, we need to adapt and change even when it is painful. We simply cannot afford to freeze.

If I were still employed full-time in the field of astronautics and insisted on using only a slide rule, I would not only be the object of ridicule, but I would be out of a job. No moral value is attached to such a choice, it is simply a matter of relating to and working in the real world.

Until I was fourteen years old, my mother used only a wood or coal burning stove on which to cook. As soon as she could afford an electric range she bought one. She welcomed the change.

In my small Iowa town of Garden City our telephone number was a single digit, 9. Today in most rural areas, phones have ten digit numbers and are fax and electronic mail capable.

These are obvious changes that most of us receive with approval and appreciation. However, there are areas where failure to change results in disaster. When our thinking freezes, when we refuse to grow and learn, or when prejudices rule our minds, we encounter great danger.

Freezing in Our Thinking

As we grow older, we may jokingly say, "Two of the things I hate to lose are my mind . . . and I can't remember the second one." A mind is a terrible thing to lose. Those whose loved ones have sunk into the abyss of old age dementia know the sorrow of losing the person they love while they still live. The tragedy is when we close and freeze our minds for no physical reason and do not recognize the problem. We then suffer a mental hardening that has nothing to do with blood circulation.

As I grow older and continue to play handball, I find that my muscles are not as resilient as they were in my younger years. I pull and strain muscles I hardly knew I had. I lose the ability to reach for certain shots. I find my flexibility has diminished. My solution is, of necessity, to regularly stretch my muscles to improve my flexibility and to prevent injury. I also find I need potassium supplements to keep my muscles from painful cramping. I must carefully watch my nutritional intake for better energy. I am always looking for new ways to improve my physical stamina and health—all for the joy of hitting a little blue ball around a court.

Mentally and intellectually, the freezing process is similar. Some men refuse to listen and learn especially in areas where they feel they have competence. They refuse to allow their ideas to be challenged. Experience and knowledge blind them to new ways of thinking. Businessmen today know this is the death knell of their business.

Being closed to new ways of thinking and doing is tantamount to closing your doors.

How many times have our children said privately, "It's no use discussing it with Dad. His mind is made up." Are we men with whom discussion is futile because others know our opinions will not change? I see that pattern in myself enough to frighten me. I suspect it has been said about me.

We need to examine our patterns and habits. They are established early in life. Our culture, families, friends, and education set many of the patterns and habits. By the time we reach twenty-five years of age, most patterns are set, altering only in minor ways in succeeding years.

How can we know if we have frozen in our thinking patterns? We may wish to be open-minded and teachable, yet are uncertain if we project that attitude to others. Here are some clues to assess our thinking flexibility:

Analyze Anger at New Ideas

Do you feel yourself getting angry at new ideas or change? When someone tries to teach you, how do you respond? Do you find yourself reacting negatively toward younger men and women who want to try new ideas? Or even repeated ideas that you tried and did not work for you? When that happens, watch out! Your anger is a sign of freezing.

Watch Negative and Critical Responses

Do you frequently look for the negative in a new idea? Do you excuse yourself by assuming this is a wise approach to avoid mistakes? Or could a critical spirit be a part of your personality? Negative responses often indicate a reluctance to listen and change. If negativity or criticism is frequent or increasing in your life, you may be entering the freezing stage in life. Coming from an analytical engineering background I find it easy to criticize and pick things apart. It is part of my training. Although it helps me in decision making, it hinders me in hearing new ideas that I have not helped develop.

Learn to Adapt

Many people say, I'm just too old to change and learn how to:

- use the computer
- play golf
- learn a new language
- witness for Christ
- take on a new task in church

As technological changes occur at an increasing rate, we may feel like we are far behind the learning curve. We suffer sensory overload. We resent our computer becoming outmoded in two years. We tire of trying to keep up with language changes, new products, new television programs. The changes seem unrelenting. We long for the familiar.

We do tire of change. Yet we cannot freeze the clock of progress. When we learn to accept change and adapt to it, we can make it work to our advantage as we grow in understanding. We learn to adapt. We remain fresh and vigorous in our learning processes.

Embrace the future. Embrace and evaluate what is new. Experience it. Keep what is good and discard the rest. This attitude gives evidence of a growing and vital mind.

> *We do tire of change. Yet we cannot freeze the clock of progress. When we learn to accept change and adapt to it, we can make it work to our advantage as we grow in understanding.*

Overcome a Lack of Curiosity

My grandson, Joshua, is exceptionally curious. From the time he could crawl, he has been a confirmed knob-turner, switch-thrower, see-what-it-does-if-I-push-this type of child. He thoroughly investigates anything mechanical. When he enters a room he immediately focuses on any item with moving parts or switches or handles.

Every child learns through curiosity. A child keeps learning every day—driven by curiosity. It is a shame that adults lose that childlike interest in the world about them.

I enjoy interacting with elderly people who keep their curiosity at a high level, who ask questions, who try new things. Rather than turning inward to worry about looks or health or reputation, they continue to learn and grow.

I recently visited with my former high school history teacher and his wife, Louis and Margery Livingston. They are 96 years old. We discussed world issues, current events, politics. They were vitally interested in my work. He brought his experience to bear on the current issues, including just a vague remembering of the past. It was a refreshing time. He challenged my thinking as a high school senior, and he challenges my thinking now.

> *Don't let your curiosity freeze. Become an inveterate observer. Ask questions. Keep learning. Curiosity, observation, and learning indicate your mental flexibility and provide new patterns of thinking.*

Don't let your curiosity freeze. Become an inveterate observer. Ask questions. Keep learning. Curiosity, observation, and learning indicate your mental flexibility and provide new patterns of thinking.

Be an advocate of good change.

Avoid the Personality Excuse

"Can the Ethiopian change his skin or the leopard its spots?"(Jeremiah 13:23). One of my nightmares is that my children, grandchildren, or coworkers will say, "Don't bother talking to him. That's just the way he is. He's got his mind made up and he won't change."

Sadly, that is probably true to some extent. I am stubborn. And I know stubbornness is no virtue. I know that I have a certain personality, verified by more psychological profiles and tests than I care to count. I also know how difficult it is to change the basic aspects of my personality.

From young adulthood on, our personalities with their quirks, foibles, imperfections, and virtues seem to harden. We hold high respect for people who continue trying to change. Too often we say, by word or actions, "This is the way I am. Accept me as I am because I can't, I won't, change."

An acquaintance, with a reputation of being a curmudgeon, usually wearing his undershirt with shorts told me, "If they're my friends, they won't care. If they're not my friends, I don't care." Such an attitude will isolate us and eventually kill our spirits. We violate a key law of mental survival—the willingness to change.

Changing and developing are firm principles of the new birth. God can change any aspect of our personality that needs changing.

The apostle Paul makes an assessment for believers: "Therefore, if anyone is in Christ, he is a new creation; the old has gone, the new has come!" (2 Corinthians 5:17). Changing and developing are firm principles of the new birth. God can change any aspect of our personality that needs changing.

The introvert can learn to be more outgoing. The voluble and sociable can learn to guard the tongue. The critical can learn to avoid cutting, hurtful comments. The quick tempered can learn to curb anger. We can choose to change.

We are in great danger of freezing when we think, "That's just the way I am." We can avoid that danger by thinking, "My personality is there for God to mold, change and use."

Evaluate Prejudices

Prejudice exists in every part of the world. Color, race, language, looks, family background, wealth, and education all provide breeding grounds for prejudice. It is a poison that begins when we are small children and destroys us as adults.

We understand prejudice intellectually. But inwardly we still fight the bigotry we collected in our family and community. As we grow older our prejudices harden and develop in subtle ways.

Hopefully, we subdue and obliterate the more heinous biases of race, gender, and nationality. Other biases creep in and we develop new prejudices that we try to express as "convictions." Occasionally, we even appeal to the Bible, as many people did during the days of slavery.

We express some of these prejudices in our views of music, hair styles, worship formats, dress fashions, politics, social issues, or personal activities. What we think are convictions are really prejudices when we have no sound biblical foundations for them. Prejudice judges and condemns others. Prejudice says, "I know better. I am right."

> *All of us carry prejudice, both known and unrecognized. The key is to keep from freezing in these prejudices, to uproot biases that are unbiblical, and to learn to change the way we think.*

Much prejudice results from our upbringing and our early environments where we develop ideas without foundation, opinions without reason, judgments without mercy, feelings without fact.

All of us carry prejudice, both known and unrecognized. The key is to keep from freezing in these prejudices, to uproot biases that are unbiblical, and to learn to change the way we think. When we see ourselves becoming more opinionated, critical, and inflexible in our thoughts, we are in danger of freezing in our prejudices.

Stages of Adult Development

To live, one must grow and keep on growing. It is an axiom of life. Studies have shown that when men retire, they are likely to die within a few years unless they keep interested, active, and growing. The moment we stop growing intellectually and personally, we begin dying. Sadly, this can happen at any age. We can "freeze" in our youth.

The wise counselor of Proverbs says: "Let the wise listen and add to their learning, and let the discerning get guidance" (Proverbs 1:5). "If you love learning, you love the discipline that goes with it—how shortsighted to refuse correction!" (Proverbs 12:1, MSG). "Wise men and women are always learning, always listening for fresh insights" (Proverbs 18:15, MSG).

I see patterns in the decades of life. We categorize the "Terrible

Twos" and other developmental ages for children, and we can do the same for adults.

- 20-30 Age of Learning
- 30-40 Age of Accomplishment
- 40-50 Age of Relearning
- 50-60 Age of Learning and Growing or Freezing and Dying
- 60+ Age of Character and Influence

The Age of Learning

In our twenties we prepare for life and work. Our attitude is one of learning, discovering, experimenting. Life offers opportunity and hope. We seek and accept education, experience, and training as the norm. We receive correction and counsel. In many ways, our lives are an open page waiting to be filled with life's story. It is an exciting time of life.

I experienced an insatiable appetite for learning during my twenties when I was involved in the early days of America's space program at Cape Canaveral. I found out how little I knew and hungered to grow. I sought opportunities for growth. I also saw my need to grow and change in my relationship with my family and with God. I knew I needed to change and mature. Everything was a challenge and a door to the future.

The Age of Accomplishment

In our thirties we see more clearly what we can do. We apply ourselves to the task. We have strength, will, ambition, and drive. Although we still learn, our hunger for learning diminishes, replaced by ability which directly contributes to doing our task. Life becomes intense. Our children become teenagers. Our marriages fray at the edges, or break. The life of the Spirit and of reflection recedes under the necessity of survival and the drive to accomplish. Without knowing it, our learning curve narrows to the necessary.

Questions of career, family, and purpose surface momentarily but usually receive only cursory attention. Many mid-life issues begin to

We sense the need of more attention to marriage and family. We become complacent in the spiritual issues of life often due to the pressures of life. Without realizing it, our life foundations are being eroded.

emerge. We can see the potential, or lack thereof, in our job and career. We sense the need of more attention to marriage and family. We become complacent in the spiritual issues of life often due to the pressures of life. Without realizing it, our life foundations are being eroded.

The Age of Relearning

In our forties we find that we must "go back to school." Career fields change drastically and even disappear. Lack of learning and development in our thirties catches up with us in the forties. Relearning, retooling, changing careers becomes a necessity. We make the change, often out of necessity rather than desire. And we may get a new lease on life. At this point the cracks in our marriages and the needs of our children become overwhelming. The famous "mid-life crisis" hits many men with hurricane force strength.

In spite of the difficulties, the forties give us great opportunities for rebuilding the right foundations, growing the right roots in every area of our lives. Seminars on marriage and family, more education and training in our work, reading on the "how-to's" of life attract us and help us.

The early losses of life, sin, and pride have taken their toll. This is a teachable time of life. Relearning is a must but would be much easier if it were developed as a pattern earlier in life.

The Age of Learning and Growing or Freezing and Dying

The fifties may be the most critical time of all. During this period of time a man makes a choice to either freeze or grow. Doing, learning, and growing must work together. He keeps doing his work of life out of necessity. But doing is not enough. We live in a society where whole career fields disappear with regularity and new ones appear with seeming spontaneity. In an information age where knowledge multiplies astronomically in a decade, a man cannot remain stagnant and still remain competitive in his work. Learning must continue. Individual growth insures future contribution and happiness in later years.

The alternatives are frightening—freezing and beginning to die. Although learning and growth come naturally to a few, most of us must pursue them purposefully. The cliché "Been there, done that!" so easily characterizes our attitude. We grow tired. We want to relax. Change frustrates us more and more. We long for the old days.

But the past is only a memory. It cannot be recovered. Its lessons, however, can guide us to the future. "Remember all the way the LORD your God led you!" (Deuteronomy 8:3). "And the LORD is the one who goes ahead of you; He will not fail or forsake you" (Deuteronomy 31:8, NASB). "Choose you this day whom ye will serve" (Joshua 24:15, KJV).

Growth is moving from the past to the future under God's leading. Freezing is a refusal to grow and change. The results imprison us to the past.

> *"We have grasped the mystery of the atom and rejected the Sermon on the Mount. The world has achieved brilliance without wisdom, power without conscience. Ours is a world of nuclear giants and ethical infants."*
>
> GENERAL OMAR BRADLEY

The Age of Character and Influence

The sixties and beyond is the age of character and influence. But only if a man continues to grow and learn. Deciding to grow and to keep growing is a sign of maturity. This involves spiritual growth that leads to spiritual maturity, and personal growth that leads to personal maturity. Spiritual growth is clear: it means developing depth in the Scriptures, newfound obedience to God and His Word, and a deepening of character.

Personal growth is not as clear. The secular world often understands it better than the spiritual world. Are spiritual and personal growth connected? Most certainly. Personal growth without spiritual progress is empty—as is so easily seen in how the world is ruled. General of the Army Omar Bradley expressed this lack of wisdom when he said, "We have grasped the mystery of the atom and rejected the Sermon on the Mount. The world has achieved brilliance without wisdom, power without conscience. Ours is a world of nuclear giants and ethical infants."[1]

Spiritual growth without personal growth is an anomaly since true spiritual growth and maturity involves the whole person. Lack of personal and spiritual growth leaves us ineffective in influencing the world for Christ and robs us of the fullness of life God wants us to enjoy. Personal growth is the development of our mind and emotions. It allows us to see the world around us with understanding. It connects us to those without Christ. It makes us stable and complete.

The Key to Change and Growth

The secret to true spiritual, intellectual, and emotional growth is humility. A true learner's spirit is a direct outgrowth of humility.

We first learn from Christ: "Take My yoke upon you and learn from Me" (Matthew 11:29). We need to be spiritual sponges. After knowing Christ for forty years, I find a great temptation to relax and to live off my past knowledge. After all, I have done a lot of Bible study. I have wrestled with major decisions. I have tried to think through and study many areas of the spiritual life. I have come to certain conclusions.

Do I still need to study and develop? Yes, it is imperative. Who is to say I have not made significant errors in my study? Does God want to teach me more? Certainly.

I can easily fall into the trap of being the "answer man." Always having a reply to the significant questions of spiritual life. What arrogance that would be.

One man in his forties said, "There are not many people who can teach me much anymore." Any one of us can learn from the youngest and the simplest believer. The Holy Spirit gives insight to every follower of Christ. Even when I have carefully thought through issues,

I can listen and learn if I will only humble myself to do so.

I frequently need to be immersed in the Scriptures so that my spiritual life is not fed from leftovers of the past. I need to push toward God and His Word daily in devotional time and in deeper study.

Winston Churchill said, "I have a great desire to learn, but I do not like to be taught." We need an openness to be taught, by anyone. In our personal lives and in our careers, learning prevents stagnation and obsolescence. Keep the heat on! Don't freeze!

Freezing in Relationships

In addition to freezing in our thinking and willingness to grow and change, we also can freeze in our relationships.

Freezing in Marriage

In marriages, we often see relationships reduced to a minimal necessity—functional communication, a moderate amount of argument, some level of tension, obligatory sexual activity, and public togetherness. Love is still there. Commitment remains strong. Yet something has left the relationship. We stop growing. In fact we regress.

Mary and I have seen that tendency several times in our marriage. When the children were young it seemed that we lived in separate worlds, meeting at the point of crisis or necessary decisions. I was intent on work, career, and spiritual outreach. She was intent on child rearing and supporting our complex social and spiritual outreach lifestyle. We sensed stagnation in our relationship. Recognition, and some conflict, helped us work through it to keep growing.

But the problem repeats itself. It is like growing a garden. It takes constant attention or it dies or becomes choked with weeds. We have found that we regularly, at least yearly, need to assess where we are in our lives and relationship. We have found we had to reaffirm our activities and personal direction. We have tried to take time apart together just to talk and rebuild our relationship.

The danger occurs when a couple allows the stagnation to settle in and become the norm. What is the danger? It is far more than a simple dulling of the relationship. If not heeded it can lead to divorce or, at the least, a disastrous pattern for children to observe and imitate.

> *It is like growing a garden. It takes constant attention or it dies or becomes choked with weeds. We have found that we regularly, at least yearly, need to assess where we are in our lives and relationship.*

Freezing in Other Relationships

Other relationships can also be damaged. We easily fall into patterns with our children, relatives, and close friends. You can imagine the conversation that our relationships are reduced to. How is the weather? How are the kids? What's been happening? How were the holidays? Then . . . silence. Well, we'll talk later.

Does that sound familiar? It does to me. I've done it many times. In some relationships it is sufficient. But if that is the pattern with important relationships with children or good friends, freezing is already happening. The remedy cannot be abrupt or instantaneous in reviving the relationship. Simply begin to go beyond the routine and mundane. Give them some extra time and attention. Open yourself up a little. Share more of what is going on inside you. Work at transforming your relationship with your children according to their ages. If they are now adults, move to a more adult friendship, not just a parental relationship that got stuck in the strained communication of their teens.

One last thought about areas that freeze. Some of us may be "stuck" in patterns of sin. If you recognize areas like this in your life, I encourage you to go back and review the discussion in chapters nine through fourteen. One of the central reasons for freezing in our minds and relationships is becoming bogged down by persistent sin in our lives. When that happens we certainly find it difficult to grow and develop in other areas of our lives.

Thawing Out from the Freeze

Several times in my life I have been outside in bitter cold weather. Almost without knowing it, my fingers, toes, face, and ears were numb with near frostbite. When I came back to the warmth of my house, my body began to thaw. As it thawed, pinpricks of intense pain appeared all over. However, I knew it was temporary. I needed to endure the pain as life-giving blood flowed back into the surface of my skin. Thawing from the freezing in many areas of life is a bit like that—some pain in the process. Yet we must know that the pain is well worth the result, even necessary, to revive the whole.

I want to encourage you that the effort you give to growing in all these areas will result in such a greater joy in life that our pain will soon be forgotten.

Larry Crabb expresses it well:

> Life can be tough. And godly people will feel its impact. . . . When bad passions seem to have the upper hand, we must remind ourselves that God is working to entice us with the prospect of knowing him, and he is appealing to parts of our souls that are not drawn to lesser pleasures. And these parts define who we really are as Christians.
>
> God's method of drawing us closer to him is to disrupt the fallen structure by allowing us to feel the terror and pain the structure was designed to overcome. He then entices us with the hope of finding in him the satisfaction of every noble desire.[2]

We do find that hope and satisfaction as we step into the unfrozen future.

QUESTIONS FOR THOUGHT AND DISCUSSION

1. Describe some people you know who have "frozen."

2. What helps people grow and develop mentally?

3. Where do you need to grow?

4. What prejudices do you see coming from your family background and upbringing?

5. Consider the ages of learning in this chapter. Do they match your observations? Where are you now?

6. What motivates you to keep growing and changing? What is wrong with not growing and changing?

SCRIPTURAL INSIGHTS:

1. List some of the changes Moses had to make in his life (see Exodus). Did he change willingly? What can you learn about change from him?

2. What do 2 Corinthians 5:17; Proverbs 1:5, 12:1, and 18:15 teach you about change?

THE DANGER
OF CONFUSION

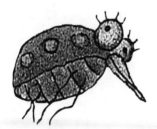

CHAPTER SIXTEEN

THE DANGER OF CONFUSION IN LIFE

I was driving alone at night in Birmingham, England. I was lost. Perhaps not really lost, since I had some idea where I was. I recognized none of the street names. I couldn't tell if I was going towards or away from my destination.

I started down one street. After a mile I knew it was wrong. I went back to where I started and tried another route. I realized I was thoroughly confused. While I was trying to remember to drive on the left, to give way on the roundabouts, and generally not to do something stupid, I *felt* stupid. I knew I was close, but I was disoriented. After further trial and error, I finally arrived at my destination.

When I drive in a strange city, I know I will eventually figure out the right route, but the process of wrong turns, misjudgments, and confusing streets becomes very frustrating. I soon forget the new sights around me and become totally absorbed in finding my way.

Life is like that, often at the most inconvenient of times. One of the most disconcerting feelings a man can have is confusion. Men want to know where they are going and how to get there without asking for directions. Uncertainty troubles us. We want to be responsible and directed.

All men will face confusion at some point in their lives, probably at several points in their lives. Like many other dangers described earlier, confusion sneaks up and catches us unaware. We are traveling comfortably down a pathway and suddenly find the way obscured. A fog sets in and we cannot see clearly. Our thinking processes get muddled. Our ability to make decisions seems blocked. We are not just lost looking for the right road, we don't even know where we want to go.

This confusion often results in divorce, escape into alcohol, a revived adolescence, depressing career changes, loss of motivation, or spiritual rebellion.

If you have been through it or are experiencing it now, you recognize immediately what I am saying. If you haven't experienced confusion, you are probably thinking, "That won't happen to me." But it will.

We used to call this confusion a "mid-life crisis." It is more than that. It can occur at any time, at any age. And it's dangerous.

Gail Sheehy calls this "middlescence, adolescence the second time around. Turning backward, going around in circles, feeling lost in a buzz of confusion and unable to make decisions."[1]

Growth and Change Breed Confusion

Men, and women too, face confusion at several points in their lives.

In the teens: Who do I want to become? What do I want to do? What kind of character do I want? I've got to stop playing and start working, but working at what?

Young adulthood and early marriage: How can I balance the

demands of wife, children, and career? Have I chosen the right career? I'm not sure I like my work all that much.

In the middle years: How can I handle this crisis with teenagers? What about job disappointment, job loss, strained marriage? I'm troubled by my decreasing physical prowess.

In the fifties: Why do I have so many physical problems? How can I handle this dead-end career and all of the financial pressures? I am fearful of retirement and the empty nest. My marital stress is heavy.

Robert Hicks, in his discussion of the stages of manhood, says, "Others may struggle more with the confusion that confronting their own mortality can bring. Still others may have difficulty accepting the fact that many of their unfulfilled yearnings will never be satisfied."[2]

Then he speaks of the life process, "Confusion is normative for the masculine journey as you move from one stage to another. Don't let the confusion be a problem for you. This is transition time, and transitions always breed confusion."[3]

Confusion is a normal experience, fraught with many dangers and detours. The clarity and direction that come into focus as we emerge from confusing periods of life are well worth the trip.

Earlier I spoke of inevitable losses. These losses cause us to think differently, or to stop thinking logically. We either directly or vaguely entertain questions like:

- Who am I?
- Why am I in this marriage?
- Why didn't I get promoted?
- Why haven't I realized my dreams?
- What will I do if "this" does not work out?

> *"Confusion is normative for the masculine journey as you move from one stage to another. Don't let the confusion be a problem for you. This is transition time, and transitions always breed confusion."*
> ROBERT HICKS

- Why did I get divorced?
- Do my children love and respect me?
- Why was I unfaithful?
- Why am I dependent on alcohol?
- Why am I not happy now that I've achieved my goals?

In wrestling with these questions we become vulnerable, unstable, perplexed. Yes, confused.

Two speeding trains seem to hit us at once. I express them here as *calling* and *major life issues*. Calling involves a combination of vocation and the spiritual elements of our lives. Major life issues reflect the events and circumstances that face us all—marriage, children, death, finances and health. Let's examine them.

Calling and Vocation

Life is work for most men. Our identity is deeply intertwined with our work. We would deny the adage, "I am what I do," yet so much of a man's existence is consumed by work. His livelihood depends on work. His self-image focuses largely on how his work is progressing.

Calling and Career

Certainly, he cares about his wife and children. But to support them he needs to work. He has other drives—sports, hobbies, relationships, and travel—but work dominates. In the early stages of a man's life, his job and career capture most of his thoughts.

Inevitably, this centeredness on work is invaded by confusions. *Job satisfaction* starts to fray. Most jobs lose their luster as one settles into routine and reality. We become unsettled, looking for a new challenge, higher pay, a better company, or some element of enjoyment in work that has eluded us in our current job.

Some men stay in a less-than-satisfying job simply because they must. Tenure, education, age, or finances prohibit a job change. Then image and identity begin to crack. The engineer thinks he really wants to be an artist. The construction worker finds he wants a college degree. The teacher tires of children and wants to be in business.

The lack of satisfaction brings us to confusion and decision. The risk of change is great, so many men choose to live in the confusion, unwilling to move to a new focus.

A *job change* can lead to confusion or new encouragement. Often a job change is forced upon us. The company transfers us. Our position "disappears." We move for the sake of our family. When such a change is strictly of our own choosing, we do well. But when we are "forced" to change by external circumstances, then confusion and disorientation often develop.

Joseph, the son of Jacob, had a slight job change thrust upon him (Genesis 37-45). He went from being his father's favorite son and in a position of privilege to being a slave in Egypt. Then as he worked his way to the top of Potiphar's household staff he was falsely accused and thrown into prison. Talk about confusion! Yet he always set about to make the best of his circumstances.

I have known men who had to take less of a job than they wanted and were trained for. Some spent years in discouragement or confusion. Others set out to make the best of it, sensing God's hand in the circumstances.

> *When we are "forced" to change by external circumstances, then confusion and disorientation often develop.*

Job jeopardy is even more confusing. Downsizing, performance reviews, and competition can put our jobs in danger. Many men are living month by month, not knowing if they will have a job. For men in seasonal or project work, that threat is always there. The tension of our uncertainty and vulnerability leads to confusion and stress. Our egos and sense of value get damaged. We feel like a piece of property in the job market.

This is the confusion:

- Am I valuable?
- Am I expendable?
- Am I competent enough to be wanted?

When a job is seemingly secure, then the drive for *job success* takes over. Success is such a relative concept. It's measured largely by our past and our peers.

Since I travel frequently in poor countries, I see that for many, just having employment and getting paid is success. But for most of us in the Western world, we see success as increasing pay scales and promotions. We have expectations of ourselves which drive us.

Unfortunately we will "max out." At some point, early or later in life, we will view ourselves as having failed. It is at that point that we become confused. Did I pick the wrong career? What if I had done this or that, would I have been more successful?

> **When men are quite successful, some will discover it to be an empty achievement, particularly if they achieve it at the expense of their family or their spiritual lives.**

There is another side to the success concept. When men are quite successful, some will discover it to be an empty achievement, particularly if they achieve it at the expense of their family or their spiritual lives. Then they enter a time of regret and confusion. Was it worth it? What did it cost me? Is this all there is to it?

The Other Calling

For the lay believer, call has usually meant "vocation." The "other calling" many recognize is the calling to spiritual or religious service. This division does great disservice to the layman.

Every believer in Christ has, or should have, a spiritual calling. We each have gifts and talents from God which He wants us to use to the maximum. Most men use their gifts and talents in the secular marketplace.

In the spiritual realm, men usually engage in a "grab bag" approach to their efforts, giving themselves to whatever is needed, available, or requested. This results in most men functioning spiritually outside their gifts. Also, it results in men doing too many things. Of course, some men do nothing in the spiritual realm, resulting in great poverty of spirit. This lack of focus leads to discouragement and confusion, not only in spiritual endeavors, but in life.

Every person is called spiritually, not just pastors or vocational

Christian workers. But most men have not clarified that calling or have not acted on it. Only when our spiritual calling and vocational calling are in balance does our confusion begin to disappear.

The Keys to Conquering Confusion

Gail Sheehy describes the fifties for men as the "Flaming '50s or Flameout." I have seen both. Some men thrive, others thrash about, never coming to a sense of direction for their lives.

Sheehy describes men at this passage as "disillusioned about themselves or having to adjust their aspirations downward."[4] What do men worry about? Losing hair and decreasing ability in sports! She points out that men who see themselves on the downside of a career "become frustrated and depressed and feel worthless, *no matter what they have achieved up to that point.*"[5] This leads us to consider two keys to overcoming or avoiding confusion.

Surrender

No one likes to give up. There is something in the male ego that hates quitting. We want to conquer, to succeed. When a person surrenders in human terms, such as to the law, it means giving up freedom to do as you wish and to follow or go according to the will of another. We do this regularly in marriage, surrendering what one wants to the needs and wishes of one's wife. We do it at work, obeying the directions of an employer.

In the life of a believer in Christ, surrender means to turn your life unreservedly and irrevocably over to Him. That is what Jesus means when He says, "If anyone would come after me, he must deny himself and take up his cross daily and follow me" (Luke 9:23). I like the phrasing in *The Message*, "Anyone who intends to come with me has to let me lead. You're not in the driver's seat—I am. Don't run from suffering; embrace it. Follow me and I'll show you how."

In Jesus' discussion on Lot's wife (who looked back on her cherished life in Sodom and turned into a pillar of salt), He said, "Remember what happened to Lot's wife! If you grasp and cling to life on your terms, you'll lose it, but if you let that life go, you'll get life on God's terms" (Luke 17:32-33, MSG).

That is surrender, having life on God's terms. He wants us to surrender to His sovereignty in all our circumstances, even in our confusion. This is surrender to:

- where God put me;
- who I am;
- my past;
- my gifts.

The way through the fuzz of confusion is to surrender your will to God for anything He wants you to do. This means submitting to God's authority and plan for your life.

Many times in my life I was not really pleased with the plans God had obviously brought my way. When our 30-year-old son was murdered, I entered a period of confusion. What is God doing? Why? Why Steve? The haze of the succeeding months was too thick, seemingly impenetrable. I thought I would never emerge from the grief and confusion.

Only as I began to submit and surrender to God in these terrible circumstances did peace and focus return. In fact, the focus of my life became much more clear. I realized that many of my previous motivations were tainted with pride and ego.

I remember other times when my job was not going as well as I expected. I struggled with what I should do about criticism and conflicting counsel regarding my leadership in The Navigators. I was urged to lead with stronger authority, but I had no peace (or was it courage?) to do that. I chose to wait—a very difficult thing for me since I am a doer and activist.

There were periods of confusion as to whether I was doing right. It took a couple of years to confirm the direction I felt God had led me. Gradually, the confusion cleared and I was confident of God's direction. But I had to surrender myself, my reputation, and my own tendencies.

It is always easier to look back on the struggles of confusion with 20/20 hindsight. But in the midst of these events, life was not so clear. If you are in a period of confusion, I urge you to surrender to God and then to *wait*. Wait for Him to clarify your direction. Don't act hastily on a job change, a divorce, a lawsuit, a move, or a large financial commitment. Let the confusion dissipate, then act.

> Yet the LORD longs to be gracious to you;
> he rises to show you compassion.
> For the LORD is a God of justice.
> Blessed are all who wait for him!
> (Isaiah 30:18)

When Job was struggling in his confusion and arguing with God about his condition, God replied, "And it is even more false to say he doesn't see what is going on. He does bring about justice, at last, if you will only wait" (Job 35:14, TLB).

Like surrender, waiting is difficult. It is one of the most significant expressions of faith. We ask our children to wait for dessert or to wait for the weekend for a special activity. They do wait, partly because they have no choice, but also because they trust us to be true to our word. So God will be true to His word as we wait.

Oswald Chambers, my favorite devotional author, speaks of both surrender and waiting:

> There is only one thing God wants of us, and that is our
> unconditional surrender. . . . Have we come to the place
> where God can withdraw His blessing and it does not affect
> our trust in Him? When once we see God at work, we will
> never bother our heads about things that happen, because we
> are actually trusting in our Father in Heaven whom the world
> cannot see.[6]

> Wait on God and He will work, but don't wait in spiritual
> sulks because you cannot see an inch in front of you! Are we
> detached enough from our spiritual hysterics to wait on God?
> To wait is not to sit with folded hands, but to learn to do
> what we are told.[7]

So we surrender and wait. . . .

Clarify Your Life Message

Although we choose to surrender to God and to wait for Him, there is another avenue He wants us to pursue to clear up our confusion.

When we are young we generally pursue a number of interests, trying to find out what we do well and enjoy. As we go on in life we discover our abilities and talents and try to focus on using them. We are privileged to live in a country and time of history where it is fairly easy to change jobs and even careers. Much frustration in work results from the failure to match our jobs with our talents and abilities.

> To wait is not to sit with folded hands, but to learn to do what we are told.
>
> OSWALD CHAMBERS

But our work is not who we are, in spite of being pigeonholed by the kind of job we have. What do I really want to be known for? A good father? A faithful husband? A man of integrity? A generous man? Love for God? My political views? In short, what is my *life message*, or my life mission?

The concept of a life message is an understanding of the combination of my spiritual and vocational calling. It could be answered by responding to the questions, "What drives me? What am I motivated to do?" When you think of a famous person you automatically consider his or her life message. For Billy Graham, it is evangelism. For Mother Teresa, it is compassion for the helpless. For John D. Rockefeller, it was money and business. For Muhammad Ali, it was being the greatest in boxing. You can think of many others whose messages include money, power, a beautiful house, success, winning, or being the best at something. Others have no message at all. When you think of them there is no distinguishing drive to their lives.

I love to play handball. But that is not what I want to be known for (not much chance, considering my level of play!). I hold rank in the Air Force Reserve, but I don't want to be remembered primarily as a general. That becomes quite empty in real life meaning.

A life message is something that God brings out in our lives as we grow spiritually. All other areas of our lives—our jobs, homes, lifestyle, accomplishments—become a vehicle for that message.

THE DANGER OF CONFUSION IN LIFE 165

The apostle Paul expressed it when he said, "This one thing I do" (Philippians 3:13, KJV), or as The Living Bible expresses it, "I am bringing all my energies to bear on this one thing." Paul said, "I press toward the mark for the prize of the high calling of God in Christ Jesus" (Philippians 3:14, KJV). Paul knew where he was going and why he was going there. The passion of Paul's life was to serve God and to bring the gospel of Christ to the world.

> *If you are in a period of confusion, I urge you to surrender to God and then to wait. Wait for Him to clarify your direction. Don't act hastily.*

To be meaningful, our life message needs to be rooted in God and His call to us. Everything else is secondary. This does not at all imply being full-time vocational Christian workers. *It does mean being driven by what is on God's heart for us.*

The context of this discussion is confusion. Knowing our life message or life direction is key to bringing order out of our confusion. Another way to phrase this question is, "What is my primary ministry and purpose?" For some people it has been helpful to develop a personal mission statement much as we would do for our company, department, or church. This would involve identifying our gifts and values.

Paul Stanley and Bobby Clinton have helped me to think of "convergence" in our lives which leads to making decisions about life directions and work in light of how God has led us in the past and how God has gifted us.[8]

After many years it has become quite clear to me that I am driven by two purposes. The first is relating to people from each of the different environments of my life who do not know Christ personally, trying to communicate the gospel to them. The second is seeing believers grow to a point where they reproduce their lives spiritually, reaching and discipling others.

You might say, "What do you expect of a Navigator?" But it would be incongruous to be in The Navigators and not have my life message relate significantly to The Navigator mission. This was my passion as a layman also; I didn't adopt it just to get a job. I came to the job because this was my life message. I have occasionally been asked to be a candidate to lead other organizations. Those who tried to recruit me found it difficult to see that I was driven more by my life message than by a job responsibility.

Other purposes I have observed include prayer, evangelism, integrity in business, missions, caring for the helpless, reaching children or young teens, helping a church body develop, or teaching.

Here are some questions to help you develop your life message:

1. Am I a believer in Christ? If not, there can be no totally satisfying life message.
2. Am I trying to follow Christ with all my heart, soul, and mind? This provides the soil in which a life message grows.
3. What are my human talents and spiritual gifts?
4. What have I enjoyed doing?
5. What have I done well?
6. What have I seen God bless in my life?
7. In the spiritual realm, what drives me?
8. What opportunities do I have to serve?
9. How does my work fit in my life?
10. What do my wife and friends think drives me?
11. What has God been saying to me from His Word?

Overcoming Confusion

Sometimes our confusion is from God in order to direct us to discovering what He wants us to do. Let's not miss what He is saying to us.

Confusion reigns when we become disoriented. The classic cause for the tragic crashes of ships and airplanes is often a disorientation—not knowing where another ship or plane was. Every pilot or ship captain could tell story after story of near misses due to not knowing their precise position or altitude. In April of 1977, two 747's were taxiing in fog at Tenerife in the Canary Islands. One had to taxi on the active runway. The other inexplicably was cleared to take off. Neither saw the other. This confusion resulted in 575 deaths when they collided as the one accelerated to take off.[9]

In life, knowing where we are and where we are going erases confusion and disorientation. Knowing our calling and life message aids us through times of confusion. Simply recognizing the possibility of such confusion is a great help in overriding the resulting danger. When confusion strikes, take time to seek God, to understand more of His will for you, and to get your direction straight.

And when you have your direction follow the counsel of Jonathan Edwards: "Resolved to live with all my might while I do live, and as I shall wish I had done ten thousand ages hence."[10]

QUESTIONS FOR THOUGHT AND DISCUSSION

1. Describe your observations of men entering a period of confusion.

2. How would you describe "calling"? How does it relate to career and vocation?

3. How can you overcome confusion?

4. Discuss the concept of a "life message." What do you think yours is? If you cannot identify a life message for yourself, how can you develop one?

5. Are there benefits to periods of confusion?

SCRIPTURAL INSIGHTS:

1. Read John 20-21. After Jesus' crucifixion the disciples were confused. Put yourself in their shoes. Compare that passage with Luke 24. What was the secret to dispersing their confusion?

THE DANGER
OF WITHDRAWAL

CHAPTER SEVENTEEN

THE DANGER
OF WITHDRAWAL

A business executive was discussing the dilemma of making friends because his company moved him so frequently. He had experienced good friendships, but found it difficult to leave them when he moved. He said, "I finally solved the problem. I don't make friends anymore."

Another man began having difficulty at work and some marriage strains at home. He began to withdraw from his friends, embarrassed at his perceived failures. He didn't want to discuss them or receive advice. When he first brought up the issues to some close friends their responses were not helpful. They either rebuked him or ignored him. Trying to reach out left him discouraged, so he gradually withdrew.

Other men come to a point in their lives when something snaps spiritually. Once they were faithful to God, seemingly committed and spiritually active, but then they begin to doubt, to allow their spiritual disciplines to decrease, to give in to small sins, and finally to begin a slow withdrawal from God. They may never know the exact cause or even perceive what they are doing while the withdrawal is going on. The result is a cooled fervor for God and a consequent eroding of faith.

In each of these vignettes, the precipitating event could have begun with loss, sin, stagnation, or confusion. The result is the same—withdrawal from people who can help and withdrawal from God.

Withdrawal rarely results from a conscious decision. More often it follows a series of small steps in a wrong direction.

Withdrawal from God

"Because of the increase of wickedness, the love of most will grow cold" (Matthew 24:12). This is a frightening verse. It is like being told on your wedding day that in two years you will stop loving your wife and will be divorced. Impossible! Never! After all, you have just pledged to love "till death do us part."

The spiritual life can easily become a series of mechanical acts of service and activities. Attending church becomes a ritual, an obligation instead of an act of worship and fellowship.

The context of Jesus' statement was the end times of tribulation, war, persecution and false prophets. It makes me wonder, "Will my love for God grow cold?" I think not, yet I have seen enough signs in my spiritual life to tell me the possibility exists. Some of those signs include a mechanical response in my relationship to God, a loss of fervor for Him, and spiritual dryness.

The spiritual life can easily become a series of *mechanical* acts of service and activities. Attending church becomes a ritual, an obligation instead of an act of worship and fellowship. Daily Bible reading slips to a few times during the week, becoming perfunctory and rigid. Bible study becomes a chore. Prayer is lifeless, lacking any real connection with God.

Jan Johnson reflected this as she wrote, "I remember the day my quiet time died. After gathering all my devotional props, I settled into a terrible emptiness. I needed God as I had never needed Him before, but my regimented prayers were puny containers for my anguish."[1]

Israel's Withdrawal

Speaking through the prophet Isaiah, God told the nation of Israel that he was sick of their trite, meaningless sacrifices:

> I am sick of your sacrifices. Don't bring me any more of them. . . . Your holy celebrations of the new moon and the Sabbath, and your special days for fasting—even your most pious meetings—all are frauds! I want nothing more to do with them . . . Quit your evil ways. Learn to do good, to be fair and to help the poor, the fatherless, and widows. . . . If you will only let me help you, if you will only obey, then I will make you rich! (Isaiah 1:11,13,16-17,19; TLB)

At this time the people of Israel lived in great prosperity. But they were carrying on the forms of worship while their lives were sinful. They became so comfortable in their prosperity that their devotion to God eroded. This can happen to us. While we do the acts of devotion, we may have lost the substance of obedience—a heartfelt worship of God and the obedience that results from a true devotion, a fervor for Him.

Loss of fervor for God accompanies this "going through the motions" type of relationship to God. Fervor is a hunger and desire for God. Hunger for food is the meeting of a human physical need. It is necessary since desire for food should be the drive to best satisfy our bodies' needs, not simply to quench our hunger. This desire for food encompasses the full range of the food's qualities—appearance, taste, quality, and kind.

In much the same way, we want our hunger for God to meet a desperate need for spiritual well-being. We want fervor to preserve the very best in our relationship with Him. We want the desire to experience all there is to be experienced with God.

> *We want our hunger for God to meet a desperate need for spiritual fervor to preserve the very best in our relationship with Him.*

The Psalmist describes this hunger: "O God, you are my God, earnestly I seek you; my soul thirsts for you, my body longs for you, in a dry and weary land where there is no water" (Psalm 63:1).

This psalm was written when David was in trouble, in all likelihood when his son Absalom betrayed him and stole the throne. He knew that all he had left was God. David was desperate enough, hungry enough, to seek God.

Similarly in Psalm 42: "As the deer pants for streams of water, so my soul pants for you, O God. My soul thirsts for God, for the living God. When can I go and meet with God?" (Psalm 42:1-2).

To keep fervor alive we need to actively seek God. We need to thirst for Him knowing that only He can satisfy us. It is too easy to withdraw and try to satisfy ourselves or solve our problems alone.

Biblical Antidotes to Withdrawal

Periodically, we may go through a time of "spiritual dryness" where our relationship with God becomes mechanical and lackluster. What can we do before the withdrawal becomes dangerous? I have found several things which help me in a dry time.

1. *Examine your heart.* See if you are harboring known sin. If so, confess it and repent. Sin is the enemy of our relationship and fellowship with God. Hidden or secret sin is especially damaging since we know it is there, but choose to do nothing.
2. *Deal with unresolved conflict.* Is there an unresolved conflict which you have been unwilling to face? Begin a process of facing it and initiating reconciliation. When

our lives are not right with people, they tend not to be right with God.

Having cleared the air in these two areas, here are some ideas to try:

3. *Take a spiritual retreat.* Get away by yourself for a weekend. Get good rest. Take only your Bible and a few select books that spiritually encourage you. If a weekend is not possible, try a couple of successive Saturday mornings.
4. *Try spiritual reading.* If you find it difficult to read extensive portions of Scripture, read or re-read small portions of Scripture and favorite devotional books such as *Words to Winners of Souls* by Horatio Bonar, *The Pursuit of God* by A.W. Tozer, *Spiritual Maturity* by J. Oswald Sanders, *My Utmost for His Highest* by Oswald Chambers. Portions from these classics encourage my soul to hunger for God.
5. *Praise God.* Listen to praise music and sing along. Let your heart and emotions enter into your time of worship.
6. *Seek good teaching.* Attend a conference that will encourage and challenge you. How often do we get away and spend an entire weekend focused on spiritual matters? (Note: write to Glen Eyrie Conference Center for information on conferences such as this: P.O. Box 6000, Colorado Springs, CO 80934)
7. *Try spiritual journaling.* Journal some of your thoughts and reflections. If you have not done this before, an excellent resource is *Spiritual Journaling* by Richard Peace.[2]
8. *Try new approaches to prayer.* Spend extended time praying through some of the psalms. Pray with a friend or a small group. Especially pray for other people and their needs. Keep a record of your prayers and their answers.
9. *Take care of your "temple"—your body.* Increase your disciplines in the areas of exercise, sleep, and diet. When you are tired or physically unfit it makes all of life more difficult.
10. *Seek intimate fellowship.* Spend time with another man or a small group with whom you can discuss your dryness

of soul. Sometimes just talking about it will be a help.
11. *Be innovative in your devotions.* Try some new approaches in your devotional time with God. Change the time, location, or format of your quiet time. If you do not have a regular time of reading the Bible and praying, start immediately.

Finally, remember that only God can bring you out of a spiritually dry period. These activities can set the stage for Him to refresh your hunger and thirst for Him. Be patient as you work at drawing near to God rather than withdrawing from Him. It is a gradual process, seldom a sudden renewal.

Withdrawal from Relationships

The next most dangerous act of withdrawal is to withdraw from the important relationships in your life. Most men hesitate to get close

> *Remember that only God can bring you out of a spiritually dry period.*

emotionally or relationally. This attitude makes it easy to draw back when you enter difficult periods of life. Men find it simple to step into emotional isolation while at the same time continuing to function at work and even in social/spiritual activities.

Withdrawal from your family produces the greatest impact on others. Your wife will see it first. She will notice your communication closing down, even more than is normal in male communication! When you sense this happening, take it as the first sign of danger. You need your wife to walk through this time with you.

When you withdraw from your children there is little they can do. They need you. They do not understand that you have needs, feelings, and problems. Even when you feel like distancing yourself, don't.

The easiest withdrawal is from friendships with other men. You just stop taking the initiative or responding to friends' requests for time. Have you noticed yourself giving the following excuses?

- "I've got a lot going on at work."
- "I need some extra time with the family."
- "Things have really been hectic this summer. How about trying me again in a couple of months?"

These excuses will soon lead to a complete withdrawal from talking with friends, unless they sense something is wrong and pursue you.

Men tend to have very few intimate friends. Most of their friendships are shallow and activity-centered around goals, work, sports, and hobbies. In general, men tend to be guarded and protective in their relationships with other men. They want to share deeply but find it difficult.

This is a dangerous time because a man can easily find himself opening up emotionally to a woman other than his wife. This is frequently the genesis of extramarital affairs—needing someone to talk to and finding someone who will listen.

Withdrawing from friendships with other believing men closes doors to desperately needed relationships and opens doors to wrong relationships. This is a time for real accountability (discussed in chapter fourteen). It is also a time to work more diligently on building and protecting friendships with a few men.

> *Withdrawing from friendships with other believing men closes doors to desperately needed relationships and opens doors to wrong relationships. This is a time for real accountability.*

The Role of Mentors

My life has been marked by several mentors. As I reflected on this topic of withdrawal, that is, the idea of simply quitting in terms of the effort required to live life in Christ, I thought of two of those mentors.

My earliest mentors were Bob Shepler and Bud Ponten. Bob and Bud were an unlikely pair to impact my life, but they did, very deeply. Both had many reasons to quit in life, to blame God for their difficult circumstances and simply to withdraw into their own worlds. But they didn't. Instead, they reached out and influenced me and many other young men.

Bud was afflicted with cerebral palsy from birth. His face was contorted. His legs required braces and his walk was jerky and ungainly. His condition required the utmost discipline and concentration from him in order to write and perform manual tasks because his fingers and hands responded so slowly.

When Bud was a teenager, his speech could barely be understood, so he sang hymns to practice his diction. Everything he did took great effort.

Bud and Bob and a few other businessmen began a Sunday school in our post-World War II neighborhood where there was no church. Both men taught my Sunday school class at one time or another. But there was much more interaction than merely a class.

Bud taught me to play tennis. He taught me to work in his print shop. He hauled me around in his station wagon to many activities. It would have been easy to withdraw from Bud or to be uncomfortable around his disabilities. But I knew he really loved God and he loved kids. He was determined to make his life count for God. It would have been easy for him to withdraw to a life of self-pity and limited relationships.

Bud remained my friend for his entire life. He encountered great difficulties throughout life. His one-man print shop finally could no longer compete against the big businesses. His body started breaking down. He developed problems in his neck, back, and ankles due to his struggle to walk. In his later years he was in constant pain.

Bud was a man of the Word and a man of character. I visited him in the hospital as he lay dying of cancer. As hospital attendants were wheeling him to the operating room for surgery, I met him in the corridor.

He said, "Jerry I've had a wonderful life! All this pain will have been worth it if it helps my children walk with Christ!"

A *wonderful* life? I had known Bud to have only pain and difficulty. Yet he never complained, even when he was discouraged. And I *never* heard him complain about his physical afflictions. He was a testimony of faithfulness in adversity.

Bob Shepler was afflicted with rheumatic fever when he was in high school. It took him six years to complete high school. That did not keep him from taking a wild bunch of young boys to the mountains for camping, fishing, swimming—all strenuous activities that boys like to do. He was always a hard worker and a demanding businessman. I also worked for Bob while I was in high school—he taught me people, business, and work skills.

Through the years I saw him begin to use a cane, then one crutch, then two crutches, and part-time in a wheel chair. When I saw him very recently he was fully confined to a wheelchair. But it is motorized and he keeps going at age seventy-seven. He is still active and creative. He won't quit. It was in the context of Bob's Sunday School class that I came to Christ. He recruited college students to help him reach out to kids. One of those students was Walt Nelson (now Dr. Walter Nelson, Professor of Education at California State Northridge). Walt prayed with me to receive Christ after one of our many outings with the class.

If anyone ever had a reason to quit and withdraw, Bob and Bud did. But they kept going and kept reaching out. They had purpose and focus. I am not naive enough to think they didn't have some significant bouts of discouragement and questioning God. But they did not withdraw.

Whenever I am tempted to quit or to withdraw, I think of them. Where would I be if they had chosen to sulk and feel sorry for themselves rather than reaching out to kids?

Never, Never, Never Give Up
Jack Canfield and Mark Hansen in their book *A Second Helping of Chicken Soup for the Soul* record the lives of many people who could have quit, but didn't. Here is a sampling:

> After years of progressive hearing loss, by age 46 German composer Ludwig van Beethoven had become completely deaf. Nevertheless, he wrote his greatest music, including five symphonies, during his later years.
>
> Wilma Rudolph was the twentieth of twenty-two children. She was born prematurely and her survival was doubtful.

When she was 4 years old, she contracted double pneumonia and scarlet fever, which left her with a paralyzed left leg. At age nine, she removed the metal leg brace she had been dependent on and began to walk without it. By thirteen she had developed a rhythmic walk, which doctors said was a miracle. The same year she decided to become a runner. She entered a race and came in last. For the next few years every race she entered, she came in last. Everyone told her to quit, but she kept on running. One day she actually won a race. And then another. From then on she won every race she entered. Eventually this little girl, who was told she would never walk again, went on to win three Olympic gold medals.

"My mother taught me very early to believe
I could achieve any accomplishment I wanted
to. The first was to walk without braces."

Louis L'Amour wrote over 100 western novels selling over 200 million copies. He received 350 rejections before he made his first sale.[3]

D. H. Groberg in his poem "The Race" describes a young boy who ran a race, falling many times, yet finishing. He wrote in one stanza,

And to his dad he sadly said,
"I didn't do too well."
"To me, you won," his father said.
"You rose each time you fell."[4]

Don't quit! Don't withdraw from God or friends! Never give up! Keep going! With God's help, you can!

QUESTIONS FOR THOUGHT AND DISCUSSION

1. Why is withdrawal a problem for men?

2. Discuss the connection between withdrawal from people and withdrawal from God.

3. Describe times when you have had fervor for God. How do you maintain this fervor?

4. Reread the biblical antidotes to withdrawal. Which ones have you tried? Which ones were most effective? What may be missing for you?

5. When you withdraw, who is hurt?

6. Have you ever had a mentor? What difference did that make in your life?

SCRIPTURAL INSIGHTS:

1. Read Genesis 3:1-13, Jonah 1–2, and Psalm 139:7-12. What do you learn in these passages about withdrawing from God? Is it possible? What causes us to withdraw from God? From friends and family?

2. Read the remainder of Psalm 139. What is the solution to withdrawal?

SPIRITUAL RENEWAL

CHAPTER EIGHTEEN

SPIRITUAL RENEWAL FOR THE INNER MAN

The tragedy of life is not that one dies,
but that one dies while he still lives.
ALBERT SCHWEITZER

Do you know what the acronym ROTJ means? Retired on the Job. Have you seen someone like that? No motivation. Can't wait until the day ends. Lifeless and looking forward to getting away from work.

This happens spiritually. A spark goes out. Motivation dies. There is little interest in God, His Word, fellowship with believers, or growing spiritually. People do not choose to grow dull in their spiritual lives. It just happens, often through encountering the dangers we have been discussing—loss, sin, freezing, confusion, or withdrawal. Whatever the cause, the remedy is spiritual renewal. We need a rekindling of our life in Christ, a new vitality, a rebirth of spiritual fervor.

The paintings of Michelangelo in the Sistine Chapel in Rome had become dull with soot and grime over the centuries. The once bright colors were shades of grey. Through careful experimentation, experts found that applying a paste of solvents which were allowed to dry, then carefully brushed away, allowed the colors to come to life again. If only our restoration were as simple. More is needed than a surface "fix." We need an inner restoration.

> *"Since God has so generously let us in on what he is doing, we're not about to throw up our hands and walk off the job just because we run into occasional hard times."*
>
> 2 CORINTHIANS 4:1, MSG

Several times my spiritual life has lost its luster and become dull. Sometimes the cause was obvious such as in the grief or depression that I have described earlier. At other times, there was no discernible cause. These were the most disturbing times. I have reflected over the years on what has helped me to be renewed. I wish I could say that there is a once-for-all solution. There is not. Renewal is a constant process, infused periodically by concentrated times of special stimulation from God.

In his own personal struggles, the apostle Paul went through many difficult times. His accounts in 2 Corinthians helped me reflect on my own spiritual renewal. He says:

> We are pressed on every side by troubles, but not crushed and broken. We are perplexed because we don't know why things happen as they do, but we don't give up and quit. We are hunted down, but God never abandons us. We get knocked down, but we get up again and keep going.
> (2 Corinthians: 4:8-9, TLB)

Paul began that chapter with the observation, "Therefore, since through God's mercy we have this ministry, we do not *lose heart*" (2 Corinthians 4:1, emphasis added). *The Message* phrases the same passage like this: "Since God has so generously let us in on what he is doing, we're not about to throw up our hands and walk off the job just because we run into occasional hard times."

We don't lose heart. We don't give up. Why? Paul explains: "Therefore, we do not lose heart. Though outwardly we are wasting away, yet inwardly we are being *renewed day by day*. . . . So we fix our eyes not on what is seen, but on what is unseen. For what is seen is temporary, but what is unseen is eternal" (2 Corinthians 4:16,18, emphasis added). In the New American Standard version, the terms "outer man" and "inner man" are used in place of outwardly and inwardly. This implies the person others see and the person you and God see.

How is this inner man renewed? God ultimately does the renewing, but there is much we can do to be fertile ground for God to work in us. The external self, or outer man becomes deeply affected by what happens internally.

The Concept of Vitality

Recently, a group of Navigator leaders from around the world met in an annual discussion of our worldwide work. We observed that some countries and individuals seemed to plateau in terms of growth, effectiveness, and fervor. A key ingredient in that plateauing, the leaders felt, was lack of spiritual vitality. But what is spiritual vitality?

Physical Vitality

I began thinking about the comparison of spiritual vitality to physical vitality. Evidences of physical vitality are resilience, energy, flexibility, and discipline. A physician will not only check for these external signs, but will also take internal "vital signs." These are heart rate, blood pressure, and possibly a range of blood and urine laboratory tests.

We have a renewed national obsession with physical health. Medical advances have greatly increased our average life span. More men and women live into their eighties and nineties. Throughout life we want to be vital physically and mentally. Health foods and exercise clubs are burgeoning industries. To live longer and healthier lives, Baby Boomers and Baby Busters and Generation Xers alike are increasingly focused on nutrition, natural remedies, and being physically fit. Why? They want to live. They want to be vital.

Since Mary's cancer, we have embarked on a significantly different eating lifestyle. We want to do our part to keep physically healthy. We find that we pay much more attention now to the basics of physical vitality. Good physical vitality then spills over into increased emotional health and vitality.

Spiritual Vitality: Renewing the Inner Life

We find similar patterns spiritually. What are the internal and external vital signs of a healthy believer in Christ? These are the keys to renewal. If we simply treat the outer disciplines, we may miss the real disease.

One morning, recently, I was looking forward to a relaxed day at work not packed with appointments. My calendar was open. Then I found that I had not recorded an early appointment, which I missed. Several other appointments were not listed in my schedule. Phone calls came in that I did not expect. The day became a nightmare. It was even worse due to my expectation of a relaxed day. Clearly, my longed-for "space" vanished.

Life never seems to turn out the way it should:

- It is harder.
- It is busier.
- Relationships are not as satisfying.
- Marriage is rarely what we expect.
- Our career seldom meets our expectations.

In short, we live life on the edge, with little or no margin. It's like the doctor who called his patient saying, "I have bad news. You have twenty four hours to live."

"Oh, that's terrible."

"But I have even worse news."

"What could be worse than having only twenty four hours to live?"

"I've been trying to call you since yesterday!"

Our lives are sometimes like that. The bad news gets worse. So often we try to solve our pressured lives with external fixes. We organize better, re-establish priorities, increase discipline, and cut out unnecessary activities. Henri Nouwen expresses what most of us feel:

> One of the most obvious characteristics of our daily lives is that we are busy. We experience our days as filled with things to do, people to meet, projects to finish, letters to write, calls to make, and appointments to keep. Our lives often seem like over packed suitcases bursting at the seams. In fact, we are almost always aware of being behind schedule. There is a nagging sense that there are unfinished tasks, unfulfilled promises, unrealized proposals. There is always something else that we should have remembered, done, or said. There are always people we did not speak to, write to, or visit. Thus, although we are very busy, we also have a lingering feeling of never really fulfilling our obligations.[1]

At the same time we are dissatisfied, we feel pulled in many different directions:

> While our minds and hearts are filled with many things, and we wonder how we can live up to the expectations imposed upon us by ourselves and others, we have a deep sense of unfulfillment. While busy with and worried about many things, we seldom feel truly satisfied, at peace, or at home. A gnawing sense of being unfulfilled underlies our filled lives.[2]

We come to the point where reorganizing is futile. We need a revolution, not reorganization. That revolution is spiritual renewal in our inner lives with God. We need a new sense of peace and purpose.

The overriding command of Christ to achieve this inner vitality is: "But seek first his kingdom and his righteousness, and all these things will be given to you as well" (Matthew 6:33).

- Seek first—our priority.
- His kingdom—what the King wants.
- His righteousness—holiness of life.
- These things—the sustenance of life.

The context in Matthew 6 is worry about our physical needs. In verse 24 Jesus says, "You cannot serve both God and Money." You cannot live with two masters. The first step in renewing the inner life is to decide to live for only one master.

But why should we make this critical decision to serve one master? It relates to the force of this verse—to seek to serve God with all our heart, soul and mind. We want to know and serve the God of Scripture. Our ultimate purpose is to become like Christ. Paul described it like this: "You are living a brand new kind of life that is continually learning more and more of what is right, and trying constantly to be more and more like Christ who created this new life within you" (Colossians 3:10, TLB).

The purpose of spiritual renewal is not just to feel better about ourselves, but to love and serve God.

Our goal is to know God more deeply as we walk with His Son daily and as we are empowered by His Spirit. He then calls us not only to His kingdom, but to a holy life. The purpose of spiritual renewal is not just to feel better about ourselves, but to love and serve God.

The Ingredients for the Renewal Process

But what is the process of inner renewal? Consider the following ingredients:

Solitude—A Place to Grow

Americans generally find silence and solitude uncomfortable. Since so much of my life is spent with people, I relish time to be alone. But to be alone and quiet without some activity to occupy my attention is not easy. I want to *do* something—read a book, make notes, listen to music, or sort through piles of papers on my desk. To just sit in solitude is difficult.

That is precisely the problem. We are so busy, so preoccupied, so frenetic, that solitude frightens us. It ought not to. We desperately need time apart to give God space and time to work in our lives.

At the beginning of Jesus' public ministry, John the Baptist was active in denouncing sin and calling for repentance. King Herod hated and feared John, "knowing him to be a righteous and holy man" (Mark 6:20,31, NASB). At his wife's instigation, Herod finally had John beheaded. This sent tremors of fear through the community, including Jesus' disciples. Sensing

Solitude does not occur naturally. It must be purposely scheduled.

this, "He said to them, 'Come away by yourselves to a lonely place and rest awhile.' (For there were many people coming and going, and they did not even have time to eat.)"

Jesus understood their need to have some space, some solitude. Even though it appears to have been short-lived, they did get away. "Come apart or you will fall apart" is a good warning.

A seed planted in the ground needs to be left alone to grow. It will die if it is constantly being uncovered to see if it is growing. Similarly, we need to be left alone to grow properly. Solitude is a place to grow.

Solitude does not occur naturally. It must be purposely scheduled. We need to come away from the rush of our lives to think, reflect, pray, and recharge. How often? How long? I cannot tell you that. It's your decision. I do not know your personality, needs, or history. But I do know that you need the solitude. You might start with a four-hour morning (evenings are notoriously injected with fatigue, interruptions, and distractions).

I recommend, after this initial short time, trying two days, easily attainable during a weekend. As I have grown older and busier, I have found that now I need about two days to unwind and only then can I get a couple of days of fruitful solitude. I'll explain more later on how to use this time of solitude. It is not just staring at a wall!

Reflection — The Essence of Cultivation
Many years ago I read a poem which mirrored my personal difficulty
with solitude and reflection.

We go, and keep on going,
Until the object of the game
Seems to be
To go and keep on going.

We do, and keep on doing,
Until we do
Without knowing — without feelings.

Is there no time to stop and reflect?
Is there no time to stop?
Is there no time?

If we stopped, would we keep on going?
If we reflected, would we keep doing
What we do?

For what we have done
And where we have gone
Is dissolved into oblivion
Or strung on the meaningless chain
Of half remembered this and that
If there is no reflection.

In all our doing have we done anything?
In all our going have we been anywhere?
(Author Unknown)

We experience both fear and anticipation in solitude and reflection.
We fear not knowing what to do and we anticipate what God can do.
We must break our cycles of busyness and relentless activity, no
matter how worthwhile the tasks we perform. What happens when
we do not take time to reflect and consider our lives?

- We suffer physically, paying the price for stress and emotional fatigue.
- Our families suffer from our lack of presence and purpose.
- Our spiritual lives suffer from not allowing God to refine our lives with Him as we reflect.

Even secular management consultants almost universally affirm the need for time away to think, reflect, and refresh. Workaholics are not productive since efficiency is dramatically reduced with long hours of work. Much has been written on the need for balance of work, rest, and recreation. People flock to semi-mystical seminars on meditation and self-development. They see their desperate need for "something" that will relieve their emotional pain and lack of fulfillment.

What do I mean by reflection and cultivation? It is simply thinking about your life and actions in light of God and His Word. It is meditating on what the Bible says. I also strongly suggest some journaling of your thoughts. Don't let that word "journaling" confuse or discourage you.

I am not talking about writing a book or *anything that anyone else will ever read.* Just jot down your thoughts. If you are wrestling with a problem, write out the facts. I find that my mind keeps chewing over anxious thoughts repeatedly. Writing them down thwarts that cycle and brings light to one's thinking.[3]

Cultivation is an agricultural word. It usually means stirring the ground around crops to let moisture and nutrients in. It also involves killing the weeds that choke growth. That is exactly what happens spiritually.

> *We have been trying to apply machine-age methods to our relations with God. We read our chapter, have our short devotions and rush away, hoping to make up for our deep inward bankruptcy by attending another gospel meeting or listening to another thrilling story told by a religious adventurer lately returned from afar.*
>
> A. W. TOZER

Cultivation stirs up the good crop and destroys the spiritual weeds that tend to choke us.

A.W. Tozer wrote:

> The idea of cultivation and exercise, so dear to the saints of old, has now no place in our total religious picture. It is too slow, too common. We now demand glamour and fast flowing dramatic action. A generation of Christians reared among push buttons and automatic machines is impatient of slower and less direct methods of reaching their goals. We have been trying to apply machine-age methods to our relations with God. We read our chapter, have our short devotions and rush away, hoping to make up for our deep inward bankruptcy by attending another gospel meeting or listening to another thrilling story told by a religious adventurer lately returned from afar.
>
> The tragic results of this spirit are all about us. Shallow lives, hollow religious philosophies, the preponderance of the element of fun in gospel meetings, the glorification of men, trust in religious externalities, quasi-religious fellowships, salesmanship methods, the mistaking of dynamic personality for the power of the Spirit.[4]

Tozer strongly urges significant times of meditation and time with God to counter this mechanized spirituality. Let's take time to reflect so that we can keep going.

The Word of God — Building Foundations

In the physical realm vitality requires a number of fundamental building blocks such as properly functioning organs, mechanically adequate joints, good general health of the body, and certainly, food which provides correct and adequate nutrition. We care for our bodies physically by supplying them with basic foods and eliminating harmful bacteria, viruses, or cancers.

Spiritually, there is one major food group — the Word of God, the Bible. The Scriptures are food for the soul. The Bible is often referred to as food, meat, water, or milk. This is terminology that everyone understands. An unalterable basic of spiritual renewal is an inner life in the Scriptures.

A healthy believer hungers for the Word. "Like newborn babies, crave pure spiritual milk, so that by it you may grow up in your salvation" (1 Peter 2:2). This is not addressed only to spiritual infants. Everyone is to have the same hunger for spiritual milk that a newborn child has for mother's milk. This milk is to be "pure," unmixed with anything. Spiritual milk isn't reading *about* the Bible or hearing sermons, but reading the Bible directly.

Milk does imply basic nutrition which must be followed by eating solid food to grow to maturity. Spiritually, it is the same:

> In fact, though by this time you ought to be teachers, you need someone to teach you the elementary truths of God's word all over again. You need milk, not solid food! Anyone who lives on milk, being still an infant, is not acquainted with the teaching about righteousness. But solid food is for the mature, who by constant use have trained themselves to distinguish good from evil. (Hebrews 5:12-14)

We need growth in our understanding *and* application of the Scriptures to be healthy, mature spiritual men. Colossians 2:7 characterizes growth as being "rooted and built up in him, strengthened in the faith."

Spiritual renewal will not come without consistent input from the Scriptures. If regular, personal study of the Word has not been the pattern of your life, it may be the missing ingredient in your renewal.

Prayer and Worship — Restoring the Soul
Worship is one of the most significant acts of a believer. Unfortunately, most people think of worship as the "morning worship service" at a church. That is not what I mean at all. As good, enjoyable, and necessary as corporate gatherings of believers may be, they are inadequate for deep spiritual renewal. Prayer and worship are needed on a personal and private basis. They are necessary ingredients in times of solitude and reflection.

Prayer and reflection will transform any dryness or intellectual study of the Scriptures. We desperately need the connection of mind and spirit. A. W. Tozer writes:

> Press on into the deep things of God. Insist upon tasting the profounder mysteries of redemption. Keep your feet on the ground, but let your heart soar as high as it will. Refuse to be average or to surrender to the chill of your spiritual environment. . . . Unless you do these things you will reach at last (and unknown to you) the bone yard of orthodoxy and be doomed to live out your days in a spiritual poverty.[5]

The tendency to view worship primarily in a church context causes me to attempt some definitions. The most literal definition of worship is reflected by the Psalmist: "Come, let us bow down in worship, let us kneel before the LORD our Maker" (Psalm 95:6).

Old Testament and New Testament words for worship mean to bow down, as to a sovereign king, and then to obey that king. The English word comes from Middle English meaning "to ascribe worth." God, as our King, asks for such a response. He wants us to submit to His sovereignty willingly and with a joyful heart. Then a major expression of that submission is obedience. In the Old Testament, people were motivated more by the fear of God than by His grace to submit to His sovereignty. In New Testament times we submit out of love, in grateful response to His mercy and grace in Christ, yet in reverent fear of God. Clearly, grace, love, and fear permeate both Testaments. In the Old Testament, God's love and grace are revealed constantly in His dealing with Israel. In the New Testament, fear is still present . . . "It is a fearful thing to fall into the hands of the living God" (Hebrews 10:31, KJV).

> *Press on into the deep things of God. Insist upon tasting the profounder mysteries of redemption. Keep your feet on the ground, but let your heart soar as high as it will.*
>
> A. W. TOZER

"Since you call on a Father who judges each man's work impartially, live your lives as strangers here in reverent fear" (1 Peter 1:17).

We often think of worship as an experience—something we do, formally or informally, to praise God or to quietly meditate on His grandeur. In addition, I see two contrasting and complementary aspects of worship:

1. To subject ourselves to the sovereignty of God.
2. To respond to God's love with adoration and praise.

Both aspects can be observed in the story of Job.

Job's response to the greatest tragedy of his life was to express his grief (tear his robe), repent (shave his head), and worship—allowing God's sovereignty to reign over every part of his life: "Then he fell to the ground in worship and said: 'Naked I came from my mother's womb, and naked I will depart. The LORD gave and the LORD has taken away; may the name of the LORD be praised'" (Job 1:20-21).

Both in public and in private we need to bow down (symbolically by kneeling or bowing) as we express our adoration and praise.

Chapters four and five of Revelation show us vivid scenes of perfect worship:

> The twenty-four elders fall down before Him who sits on the throne, and worship Him who lives for ever and ever. They lay their crowns before the throne and say: "You are worthy, our Lord and God, to receive glory and honor and power." . . . And they sang a new song: "You are worthy to take the scroll and to open its seals, because You were slain, and with Your blood You purchased men for God from every tribe and language and people and nation.". . . Then I looked and heard the voice of many angels, numbering thousands upon thousands, and ten thousand times ten thousand. They encircled the throne and the living creatures and the elders. In a loud voice they sang: "Worthy is the Lamb, who was slain, to receive power and wealth and wisdom and strength and honor and glory and praise!" (Revelation 4:10-11; 5:9,11)

This is an incredible picture of worship, which makes any expression of worship this side of heaven seem insignificant. Christ is clearly the focus, God-become-man, who was slain and lives forever. It brings to mind the Psalms, where worship is praise, singing, thanksgiving, verbal submission, and bowing down before God.

As we live in a time between Old Testament worship and this magnificent scene in heaven, what is our worship today? It certainly includes some of the same expressions of believers meeting together—praise, singing, thanksgiving, verbal submission, and bowing. Yet often the emphasis is more personal, more inward, and less formal. It takes place wherever believers are located—alone or together—not only in a temple or sanctuary. "You will worship the Father neither on this mountain nor in Jerusalem. . . . True worshipers will worship the Father in spirit and truth" (John 4:21,23).

> *Worship is attributing worth to God with reverence and awe.*

Worship is attributing worth to God with reverence and awe. We focus on God and give ourselves to Him through prayer, singing, praising and obeying—*worship in spirit.* In these activities our guide is the Scripture—*worship in truth.* These elements of prayer, singing, praise, and the Word apply both to our private worship and to worship in community (church meetings or other gatherings of believers). Perhaps we should more often physically bow down, affirming our submission to a holy God.

We have great freedom in our expressions of worship. Some prefer quietness or soft music, some celebrate with clapping and lively songs, others like the traditional liturgy. In this we learn to serve one another—new and mature believers, different cultures and customs—deferring to others' expressions as we remember that God looks on the heart.

In your solitude, learn to pray and praise in your worship. It will renew your spirit.

Fellowship and Friendship—The Encouragement Factor

We need other people. We cannot be loners and expect to grow spiritually. As much as men may think that we can get along by ourselves, we will soon wither and die spiritually. Being a believer in Christ is not an individual sport. We are connected inextricably to others in the body of Christ.

All my earlier discussions of friendship and accountability fit here. Paul found that he desperately needed others. When he was down emotionally he waited for Titus. "But God, who comforts the depressed, comforted us by the coming of Titus" (2 Corinthians 7:6, NASB). Paul needed Titus for his renewal: "Iron sharpens iron, so one man sharpens another. . . . As water reflects face, so the heart of man reflects man" (Proverbs 27:17,19, NASB). This is the same chapter that says, "A man's counsel is sweet to his friend. Do not forsake your own friend or your father's friend" (Proverbs 27:9,10, NASB). Something happens in the context of heart-to-heart fellowship.

> *We need other believers. Men especially need other men who will stimulate their soul's thirst for God.*

In Hebrews 10 our intimate relationship with Jesus and our faithfulness to Him requires us to, "consider how to stimulate one another to love and good deeds, not forsaking our assembling together . . . encouraging one another" (Hebrews 10:24-25, NASB). We need other believers. Men especially need other men who will stimulate their soul's thirst for God. Some men will make you hunger for money or success. Some will talk sports and politics making you want to learn more of these things. But we need a context of fellowship where the conversation is of important matters of the spirit.

Solitude should not replace fellowship. In fact, there are times when getting apart with two to five other people for the purpose of seeking God can be tremendously encouraging in our renewal. For instance, in a day apart, spending brief times in prayer and discussions with other men along with personal times in the Word and reflection can greatly help someone who is new at these sorts of things. I have noted an increase in people going on personal spiritual retreats with a mentor, a "spiritual director" to help them use the time profitably. Get the help you need to grow.

Inner Application—Obedience of the Heart

All this time in solitude, reflection, the Word, worship, and fellowship will be of little meaning unless there is practical application in our lives. Later we will discuss outward obedience. But outward obedience depends upon the prior application of learning what Christlikeness is to our inner person.

As adults, most of us have learned to externally control our baser instincts. We hold in our anger, guard the expression of our attitudes, and check our emotional responses. Yet our inner person may hardly change at all. The most profound effect of the Spirit's work in our life takes place in the inner recesses of our person. He wants to move us—beginning with our character and attitudes—toward Christlikeness.

> **We are to "take every thought captive to the obedience of Christ"**

The issues of sin which I discussed earlier have their roots in the inner person. Real spiritual renewal will take place when we change our attitudes of pride, egotism, jealousy, or competition. We need to change our minds, to change how we think about life, ourselves, people, and circumstances. Paul said, "Have this attitude in yourselves which was also in Christ Jesus" (Philippians 2:5, NASB). This is in the context of Jesus' lack of selfishness and conceit, His willingness to give up His own interests.

I discussed *anger* extensively earlier, so little more needs to be said. But as a reminder, since application means dealing with this Achilles heel of most men, I suggest you deal with anger at the root in your inner person.

Inner application means taking control of your *thought life*. This certainly includes thoughts of sex and lust. But it is far more than that. It includes how we think about people, circumstances, and God Himself. We are to "take every thought captive to the obedience of Christ" (2 Corinthians 10:5, NASB).

Inner application most fundamentally means listening to the Holy Spirit as you read the Word, reflect, and pray. The Spirit will point out issues in your inner life. When He does, ask God to change you, doing all you can to be obedient.

QUESTIONS FOR THOUGHT AND DISCUSSION

1. What is the "inner man"?

2. Recall a time when you experienced inner renewal. How can you tell when you need it?

3. In what ways is spiritual renewal an overall antidote to all of the dangers men face?

4. Of all the suggestions on how to pursue spiritual renewal in your inner person, which is most difficult for you? Why?

5. How important is solitude?

6. How necessary are praise and worship? What is the role of other people in your spiritual renewal?

SCRIPTURAL INSIGHTS:

1. Read 1 Corinthians 9:24-27 and 2 Peter 1:1-11. What do you observe regarding both inner and outer renewal? What is the place of discipline? What is the source of inner godliness? How does it develop?

CHAPTER NINETEEN

SPIRITUAL RENEWAL FOR THE OUTER MAN

A deep spiritual illness occurs when our inner and outer persons are incompatible. We cannot long stand the tension of believing one way and living another way. We either change beliefs to match our actions or change our actions to match our beliefs. Renewal *begins* inside our hearts. *It is completed by external conformity to God's plan for each individual.*

Inner vitality without outer vitality results in a useless life.

Biblical Clues to External Spiritual Vitality

Outer vitality without inner vitality results in a hypocritical, two-faced life.

Inner vitality plus outer vitality gives real spiritual power to our life. I do not want to invent or proscribe a checklist for external spiritual vitality, but I do believe some clues are helpful.

The epistle of James is the classic biblical statement on our external life, or good works, as it is called. The Bible speaks well for itself, so I will elaborate only briefly on the instruction of James. His basic thesis of works and faith is expressed this way:

> What good is it, my brothers, if a man claims to have faith but has no deeds? Can such faith save him? Suppose a brother or sister is without clothes and daily food. If one of you says to him, "Go, I wish you well; keep warm and well fed," but does nothing about his physical needs, what good is it? In the same way, faith by itself, if it is not accompanied by action, is dead. But someone will say, "You have faith; I have deeds." Show me your faith without deeds, and I will show you my faith by what I do. (James 2:14-18)

What can help us develop external spiritual vitality?

Develop a Heart for God

This means a godly man's desire for God is acted upon in a regular, meaningful devotional life and times of prayer: "Come near to God and He will come near to you. Wash your hands, you sinners, and purify your hearts, you double-minded. Humble yourselves before the Lord, and He will lift you up" (James 4:8,10).

In our daily times with Him we draw near to Him in the Word and prayer.

Develop Knowledge of the Word with Application

It is so easy to know the Scriptures well and still not apply them to our lives. It's what many would call hypocrisy. We want to grow deeply in God's Word, but we must also allow it to change our lives. That is what James is communicating.

> Do not merely listen to the word, and so deceive yourselves. Do what it says. Anyone who listens to the word but does not

do what it says is like a man who looks at his face in a mirror and, after looking at himself, goes away and immediately forgets what he looks like. But the man who looks intently into the perfect law that gives freedom, and continues to do this, not forgetting what he has heard, but doing it—he will be blessed in what he does. (James 1:22-25)

God has little time for the man who knows much and does little.

Control Your Tongue

The godly man controls his tongue. "If anyone considers himself religious and yet does not keep a tight rein on his tongue, he deceives himself and his religion is worthless" (James 1:26).

We all stumble in many ways. If anyone is never at fault in what he says, he is a perfect man, able to keep his whole body in check. When we put bits into the mouths of horses to make them obey us, we can turn the whole animal. Or take ships as an example. Although they are so large and are driven by strong winds, they are steered by a very small rudder wherever the pilot wants to go. Likewise the tongue is a small part of the body, but it makes great boasts. Consider what a great forest is set on fire by a small spark. The tongue also is a fire, a world of evil among the parts of the body. It corrupts the whole person, sets the whole course of his life on fire, and is itself set on fire by hell. All kinds of animals, birds, reptiles and creatures of the sea are being tamed and have been tamed by man, but no man can tame the tongue. It is a restless evil, full of deadly poison. (James 3:2-8)

We know that the mouth speaks what is in the heart. Which of us has not been deeply embarrassed by the way our words revealed our heart? Notice the passage says, "no man can tame the tongue." The implication is that only God can change us inwardly so that what comes off our tongues reveals a heart for God. Ask God to help you become such a man.

Develop Honorable Actions Toward Others

The godly man treats every person with honor and grace:

> My dear friends, don't let public opinion influence how
> you live out our glorious, Christ-originated faith. If a man
> enters your church wearing an expensive suit, and a street
> person wearing rags comes in right after him, and you say
> to the man in the suit, "Sit here, sir; this is the best seat in
> the house!" and either ignore the street person or say, "
> Better sit here in the back row," haven't you segregated
> God's children and proved that you are judges who can't
> be trusted?
>   Listen, dear friends. Isn't it clear by now that God oper-
> ates quite differently? He chose the world's down-and-out as
> the Kingdom's first citizens, with full rights and privileges.
> This Kingdom is promised to anyone who loves God. And
> here you are abusing these same citizens! Isn't it the high
> and mighty who exploit you, who use the courts to rob you
> blind? (James 2:1-6, MSG)

Have you ever been slighted or treated badly because you were a
"nobody"? The memory of that slight ought to remind us to treat
everyone as though he or she were Christ's personal representative.

Develop Humility and Christlike Ambition

The godly man subdues anger, factions, and strife in a spirit of
humility:

> Who is wise and understanding among you? Let him show it
> by his good life, by deeds done in the humility that comes from
> wisdom. But if you harbor bitter envy and selfish ambition in
> your hearts, do not boast about it or deny the truth. Such
> "wisdom" does not come down from heaven but is earthly,
> unspiritual, of the devil. For where you have envy and selfish
> ambition, there you find disorder and every evil practice.
> (James 3:13-16)

My dear brothers, take note of this: Everyone should be quick to listen, slow to speak and slow to become angry, for man's anger does not bring about the righteous life that God desires. (James 1:19-20)

What causes fights and quarrels among you? Don't they come from your desires that battle within you? (James 4:1)

Our inner spiritual lives are often defined by what causes us to get angry. Our inner lusts and ambitions become revealed by the conflicts and quarrels we generate.

Develop Resistance to Sin and Evil

The godly man actively resists sin and the evil one. "Submit yourselves, then, to God. Resist the devil, and he will flee from you. Come near to God and He will come near to you. Wash your hands, you sinners, and purify your hearts, you double-minded" (James 4:7-8). We must allow no compromise with sin. Never allow the enemy a foothold in your life and spirit, and your external walk will reflect a pure heart. This requires work and effort. We must resist, not discuss.

Develop Accountability in Relationships and Fellowship

The godly man is active in fellowship with other believers.

Therefore confess your sins to each other and pray for each other so that you may be healed. The prayer of a righteous man is powerful and effective. Elijah was a man just like us. He prayed earnestly that it would not rain, and it did not rain on the land for three and a half years. Again he prayed, and the heavens gave rain, and the earth produced its crops.

My brothers, if one of you should wander from the truth and someone should bring him back, remember this: Whoever turns a sinner from the error of his way will save him from death and cover over a multitude of sins. (James 5:16-20)

We need one another for lasting spiritual renewal.

The spiritually renewed person demonstrates discipline, good conduct, a good reputation, and a depth of knowledge of the Scripture.

Walking in the Spirit

What role does the Holy Spirit play in our spiritual renewal? The Spirit is the star, the major player. God the Father sovereignly rules over all. God the Son, sent by the Father, died for our sins and now reigns in heaven. God the Holy Spirit was sent as the invasive presence of the Father and Son in the believer. The Spirit was sent following Christ's ascension.

Many believers become uncomfortable with discussions about the Holy Spirit. Those from charismatic beliefs see the Spirit in many external signs such as tongues, healing, and prophecy. Those from noncharismatic beliefs see the Spirit in more quiet intercessory and theological ways. Either emphasis can easily miss some of the primary purposes of the Holy Spirit.

Two passages emphasize one key truth: "But I say, walk by the Spirit, and you will not carry out the desire of the flesh. . . . If we live by the Spirit, let us also walk in the Spirit (Galatians 5:16,25, NASB). "And do not get drunk with wine, which is dissipation, but be filled with the Spirit" (Ephesians 5:18, NASB).

Clearly, we are to walk by the Spirit, live by the Spirit, walk in the Spirit, be Spirit-filled, and Spirit-controlled. I am not naive enough to think that I can solve the conflicting views of the sign gifts of the Spirit. Nor will I try. That discussion clouds the primary thrust of the Holy Spirit's work.

Before a direct discussion of walking in the Spirit, note what the Holy Spirit has already done. We are:

- Regenerated by the Spirit.
  "Jesus answered, 'I tell you the truth, no one can enter the kingdom of God unless he is born of water and the Spirit. Flesh gives birth to flesh, but the Spirit gives birth to spirit'" (John 3:5-6).

- Indwelt by the Spirit.

"You, however, are controlled not by the sinful nature but by the Spirit, if the Spirit of God lives in you. And if anyone does not have the Spirit of Christ, he does not belong to Christ. And if the Spirit of Him who raised Jesus from the dead is living in you, He who raised Christ from the dead will also give life to your mortal bodies through His Spirit, who lives in you" (Romans 8:9,11).

- Sealed by the Spirit.

"And do not grieve the Holy Spirit of God, with whom you were sealed for the day of redemption" (Ephesians 4:30).

- Baptized into one body by the Spirit.

"The body is a unit, though it is made up of many parts; and though all its parts are many, they form one body. So it is with Christ. For we were all baptized by one Spirit into one body—whether Jews or Greeks, slave or free— and we were all given the one Spirit to drink" (1 Corinthians 12:12-13).

If all that is true, why then are we not always spiritual people? Why do we not experience life in the Spirit marked by peace, joy, hope, and love?[1] It is not all that complicated. In fact, the Scriptures are clear.

Let's consider these three phrases as keys:

- Grieve not.
- Quench not.
- Walk in.

Do Not Grieve the Holy Spirit

Look at the context of this command—and it is a command:

Therefore each of you must put off falsehood and speak truthfully to his neighbor, for we are all members of one body. "In your anger do not sin": Do not let the sun go down while you are still angry, and do not give the devil a foothold. He who has been stealing must steal no longer, but must work, doing something useful with his own hands, that he may have something to share with those in need.

Do not let any unwholesome talk come out of your mouths, but only what is helpful for building others up according to their needs, that it may benefit those who listen. And do not grieve the Holy Spirit of God, with whom you were sealed for the day of redemption. Get rid of all bitterness, rage and anger, brawling and slander, along with every form of malice. Be kind and compassionate to one another, forgiving each other, just as in Christ God forgave you. (Ephesians 4:25-32)

The context is sin! Sin grieves the Holy Spirit. A key to the Spirit-filled life is to deal quickly with any sin of the present or past, no matter how small or how great it may seem to us. When we tolerate unconfessed sin, we cause deep sorrow to the Holy Spirit.

Do Not Quench the Spirit
Again, note the context:

Be cheerful no matter what, pray all the time, thank God no matter what happens. This is the way God wants you who belong to Christ Jesus to live.

Don't suppress the Spirit, and don't stifle those who have a word from the Master. On the other hand, don't be gullible. Check out everything, and keep only what's good. Throw out anything tainted with evil. (1 Thessalonians 5:16-22, MSG)

Rejoicing, praying constantly, giving thanks, listening, and carefully examining messages from God through people, and abstaining from evil surround the warning not to smother or grieve the Spirit.

To quench is to say "no" to the Holy Spirit. I believe the Spirit is communicating to us almost continuously. Have you ever experienced that sense that you "ought" to do something—call a friend, talk to someone, drive somewhere, or do something? As we walk in the Spirit we will sense God tugging at our hearts. So often I have ignored those tugs. I didn't have time. It's not important. I'm just imagining things. We have many excuses for not listening to the Spirit's quiet whispers.

One time I left a meeting at our Glen Eyrie Conference Center. I had wanted to talk with someone afterwards, but he was busy. So I drove toward home. I suddenly had the sense that I should go back. I ignored it and drove as I struggled. I wanted to go home. Finally I turned back and obeyed the urging of the Spirit. I was able to find the person for a significant conversation.

> When we tolerate unconfessed sin, we cause deep sorrow to the Holy Spirit.

Many people have told of being wakened in the night to pray for a person or to call someone, only to find that a crisis was going on in that person's life. Many times I have been traveling by plane trying to get some work done, desperately trying to ignore my seat mate. Then God nudges me to start a conversation which leads to the person receiving Christ or sharing a deep need.

Quenching the Spirit also occurs when we are willfully disobedient to something the Scriptures clearly tell us to do.

Walk in the Spirit
The Greek word for "walk" is different in Galatians 5:16 and 5:25. In verse 16 it is *peripteo*, a normal word for walk. It means to tread all around or to walk about in the company of the Spirit to avoid being influenced by the flesh. Just as a child (or even a teenager) walking with parents is far less likely to get in trouble, so it is with our walking with the Spirit. If we are continually aware of the Spirit's presence, we will resist the flesh.

In verse 25 the word is *stoicheo*, meaning to march in rank, to keep step or to walk by rule. It is connected to the phrase "If we live by the Spirit." So we could say, *Since we have the source of spiritual life by the Holy Spirit, let us also conduct ourselves according to the rule of the Spirit.* Both The Living Bible and *The Message* give enlightening sense to this verse:

If we are living now by the Holy Spirit's power, let us follow the Holy Spirit's leading in every part of our lives (TLB).

Since this is the kind of life we have chosen, the life of the Spirit, let us make sure that we do not just hold it as an idea in our heads or a sentiment in our hearts, but work out its implications in every detail of our lives (MSG).

Again, the context is crucial. In Galatians 5:13-15, the apostle Paul speaks of our relationship to one another, loving our neighbor as ourselves. He warns against angry conflict. The text lists detailed works of the flesh—sexual immorality, witchcraft, relational sins, and bad moral conduct (Galatians 5:17-21). Galatians 5:22-23 lists the familiar fruit of the Spirit. Keeping in step with the Spirit (as the New International Version phrases it) is the key to not giving in to the fruits of the fleshly life.

Walking in the Spirit is a day by day, hour by hour, step by step relationship with the Holy Spirit.

Grieve not, quench not, walk. . . . These are the steps to walking in the Spirit. These are the keys to true spiritual renewal.

In his writings Oswald Chambers spoke often of the role of the Holy Spirit in our lives. He wrote:

The one and only characteristic of the Holy Ghost in a man is a strong family likeness to Jesus Christ, and freedom from everything that is unlike Him. Are we prepared to set ourselves apart for the Holy Spirit's ministrations in us? . . . The Holy Spirit cannot be treated as a Guest in a house. He invades everything. . . . He takes charge of everything. My part is to walk in the light and to obey all that he reveals.[2]

We Cannot Always Avoid the Dangers

We have looked carefully throughout this book at five critical areas of danger that *every man* will face. You are not exempt—neither am I. We must be on guard. Yet sometimes, each of us will fail. I've tried to remind you throughout that God can and will show any man compassion, mercy, and forgiveness when we fail, or fall, or merely slip a bit. The following story should remind us all how the renewal process can be appropriated.

One day it happened. But what was "it?" His mind wandered back over the past several years. His life as a believer began quite clearly. There was no question of that conscious decision he made to believe in Christ. He remembered the hunger for the Scriptures, for discovering this newfound faith and seeing it transform his marriage, family, and work.

Then, slowly, slowly, a deadening routine began to creep in. He kept doing all the things he knew he should—reading Scripture, church activities, a small fellowship group, and all the accoutrements of a committed believer. He couldn't quite identify when a spiritual dullness entered his life. He saw himself becoming more self-centered, more irritable, more distant in his relationships.

> *The one and only characteristic of the Holy Ghost in a man is a strong family likeness to Jesus Christ, and freedom from everything that is unlike Him.*
>
> OSWALD CHAMBERS

He noticed the excitement of a few friends who were younger in their faith. There was a fleeting thought, "I wonder where that excitement went for me?" But it was just that—a fleeting thought. He had found that if he became too introspective, too many unanswerable and troubling questions came up. He was simply too busy to let his emotions be stirred up with doubts. He lightly mentioned some of these feelings to a friend. The reply was, "Don't worry about it. You're doing OK. Just press on and trust God." Well, that was what he was trying to do, so he kept pressing on.

But, soon even his spiritual routine did not salve his conscience. He began to feel hypocritical. He was becoming like some of the back-pew church attenders he had so soundly criticized in his young fervor. He frightened himself when he recognized that he really didn't care too much about anything spiritual. After a summer hiatus from their Bible study group, he decided not to rejoin. He was busy at work. His kids needed more of his time for little league and other school activities. His quiet time became more sporadic.

He knew something was wrong. But he hadn't been unfaithful to his wife and there were no overt sins in his life. So he had kept trudging along. But it was starting to affect him emotionally. He didn't sleep well. He began to resent his wife's growing spirituality. He found himself becoming more irritable with her. He resented the "distance" between them emotionally, especially since they had prided themselves on being able to talk about anything.

Keeping in step with the Spirit is the key to not giving in to the fruits of the fleshly life.

Late in the year, he was hurriedly trying to catch up on his annual commitment, doggedly determining to read the Bible through. Suddenly, one phrase in Revelation 2:4 pierced his heart. "You have forsaken your first love." Something began to happen in his mind and heart. He didn't sleep well that night. Has that happened to me? Have I lost my first love for Christ?

He began to ask God to show him if this was his problem. As he thought and prayed over the next three weeks, several things began to become clear. He had allowed some specific issues of pride to slip into his life. Some of it was what he thought of as spiritual pride. He remembered his reaction when he did not get the promotion at work. Even though he thought he had handled it reasonably well, he now saw it had left a wound that had not healed. He remembered a resentment against God—and against a coworker who got the promotion. The Spirit of God brought several other issues to his mind. He jotted them down in the beginnings of a private journal. He prayed over each issue or incident as God brought it to his mind. He asked for forgiveness. A couple of times he even wept—not really his style.

Over the next three months he sensed signs of—well, for lack of a better term—renewal, coming into his life. He finally revealed some of this to one of his friends, whom he had been avoiding for the past year. That friend listened carefully and then said, "I've seen something slipping spiritually in your life. I didn't know what it was. In fact, you may recall that I broached the subject after a workout at the athletic club. I remember you put up a pretty clear 'No Trespassing' sign. So I just continued to pray for you that God would pursue you for whatever was needed." They agreed to meet weekly to talk and pray for a few times.

He decided finally to take a weekend away—by himself—to spend with God. He took just his Bible, his journal notes and a couple of books his friend had recommended to stimulate his thinking. It was both a struggle as well as a significant spiritual experience.

Now, a month later, he realized he was like a new man. He sensed a deeper commitment to the Lordship of Christ (discussed in *The Power of Commitment*).[3] There was a renewed love for God. "It" was really a deep spiritual renewal. And it did not happen in one day. But one day he realized that God had been faithful to him and he had responded over the period of several months. He finally felt as if he had faced several spiritual dangers and had emerged a different person.

A Final Word

Dangers abound in living out the life of Christ, but there are warning signs and help from God at every turn. We want to finish life well as men. We want to be role models to our children and to the non-believing world. We want to live in peace and joy in the midst of a world that pressures us at every point. We can avoid the dangers if we heed the signs and carefully apply the antidotes we have discussed. Have a great trip along this road of life!

QUESTIONS FOR THOUGHT AND DISCUSSION

1. How would you describe the difference between inner and outer renewal?

2. What happens when you have one kind of renewal without the other?

3. Of all the outer evidences of spiritual vitality, which is the most difficult for you to exhibit consistently?

4. Where do fellowship and accountability fit into spiritual vitality in the outer man?

5. Where are you in terms of spiritual renewal?

SCRIPTURAL INSIGHTS:

1. Read Galatians 5:16-18 and Ephesians 4:25-32. What does it mean to walk in the Spirit?

2. Discuss the three aspects: grieve not, quench not, walk in. How are they connected?

3. What are some practical steps to relate to the Holy Spirit? What will these concepts do for your inner and outer spiritual vitality?

NOTES

Chapter Three: Loss of Motivation
1. Mary White, *Harsh Grief, Gentle Hope* (Colorado Springs, Colo.: NavPress, 1995).
2. Larry Crabb, *Finding God* (Grand Rapids, Mich.: Zondervan, 1993), p. 174.

Chapter Seven: Loss of Confidence
1. Louis L'Amour, *The Walking Drum*, Reader's Digest, July 1995, p. 168.

Chapter Eight: The Antidote for Loss
1. J. Oswald Sanders, *Spiritual Maturity* (Chicago: Moody, 1962), pp. 35–36.
2. Alexander Whyte, as quoted in Sanders, p. 41.

Chapter Ten: When Sexual Temptation Becomes Sin
1. Robert Hicks, *Masculine Journey* (Colorado Springs, Colo.: NavPress, 1993), p. 65.
2. Hicks, pp. 58,69.
3. Jerry White, *Honesty, Morality and Conscience* (Colorado Springs, Colo.: Nav-Press, 1996), p. 180.
4. Robert Hicks, *Masculine Journey* (Colorado Springs, Colo.:NavPress, 1993), pp. 65–66.
5. Robert Daniels, *The War Within* (Wheaton, IL.: Crossway Books, 1997).
6. Chuck Swindoll *Growing Strong in the Seasons of Life* (Grand Rapids, Mich.: Zondervan, 1994), pp. 94–95.

Chapter Eleven: When Conflict Becomes Sin
1. Elliot Engel, "Of Male Bondage," *Newsweek*, June 21, 1982, p. 13.
2. Robert Hicks, *The Masculine Journey* (Colorado Springs, Colo.: NavPress, 1993), p. 76.
3. Hicks, p. 78.
4. Ken Sanders, *The Peacemaker* (Grand Rapids, MI: Baker Books, 1990).

Chapter Thirteen: When Pride Becomes Sin
1. Oswald Chambers, *My Utmost for His Highest* (Nashville: Discovery House Publishers, 1992).
2. Larry Crabb, *Finding God* (Grand Rapids, Mich.: Zondervan, 1993), p. 112.

Chapter Fourteen: The Antidote for Sin
1. C.S. Lewis, *Mere Christianity* (New York: Macmillan, 1960), p. 153.
2. Fred Hignell, III, "Sharing the Paddle," *Moody Monthly*, July/Aug. 1996, p. 51.
3. Patrick Morely, *The Man in the Mirror* (Brentwood, TN: Woglemuth & Hyatt, 1989), p. 274.
4. Morely, p. 277.
5. Morely, pp. 280-288.

Chapter Fifteen: The Danger of Freezing
1. Dr. Richard I. Halverson, "A Response to Leadership".
2. Larry Crabb, *Finding God* (Grand Rapids, Mich.: Zondervan, 1993), p. 181.

Chapter Sixteen: The Danger of Confusion in Life
1. Gail Sheehy, *New Passages, Mapping Your Life Across Time* (New York: Random House, 1995), p. 63.
2. Robert Hicks, *The Masculine Journey* (Colorado Springs, Colo.: NavPress, 1993), p. 174.
3. Hicks, p. 175.
4. Sheehy, p. 244.
5. Sheehy, p. 271.
6. Oswald Chambers, *My Utmost for His Highest* (Nashville, Discovery House Publishers, 1992), p. 297.
7. Chambers, p. 214.
8. Paul Stanley and Robert Clinton, *Connecting* (Colorado Springs, Colo.: NavPress, 1992).
9. Gary Inrig, *Feet of Clay* (Moody, 1979), pp. 281-282.
10. Jonathan Edwards, *International Encyclopedia of Quotations* (J. G. Ferguson Publishers, 1975), p. 26.

Chapter Seventeen: The Danger of Withdrawal
1. Jan Johnson, *Enjoying the Presence of God* (Colorado Springs, Colo.: NavPress, 1996), p. 8.
2. Richard Peace, *Spiritual Journaling* (Colorado Springs, Colo.: NavPress, 1995).
3. Jack Canfield and Mark Victor Hansen, *A Second Helping of Chicken Soup for the Soul* (Deerfield Beach, Fl.: Health Communications, Inc., 1995), pp. 254-255.
4. Canfield and Hansen, p. 280.

Chapter Eighteen: Spiritual Renewal for the Inner Man

1. Henri J. M. Nouwen, *Making All Things New* (San Francisco: Harper, 1981), pp. 23-24.
2. Nouwen, p. 29.
3. See Richard Peace, *Spiritual Journaling* (Colorado Springs, Colo.: NavPress, 1995) for more specific ideas.
4. A. W. Tozer, *The Pursuit of God* (Harrisburg, Penn.: Christian Publications, 1948), p. 69.
5. A. W. Tozer, *The Root of the Righteous* (Harrisburg, Penn.: Christian Publications, 1955), p. 56.

Chapter Nineteen: Spiritual Renewal for the Outer Man

1. I am indebted to Dr. Bruce Wilkinson of Walk Thru the Bible for stimulating my thinking in these areas.
2. Oswald Chambers, *My Utmost For His Highest* (Nashville: Discovery House Publishers, 1992), pp. 39,100.
3. Jerry White, *The Power of Commitment* (Colorado Springs, Colo.: NavPress, 1986)

AUTHOR

DR. JERRY WHITE is the president and chief executive officer of The Navigators and is responsible for the worldwide operation of The Navigators. The Navigators have more than 3,650 staff ministering in 102 countries, working with college students, military personnel, business and professional people, and churches.

Dr. White was born in Iowa and raised in Spokane, Washington. He attended the University of Washington and received a B.S. in electrical engineering in 1959. In 1964 he received a Masters Degree in Astronautics from The Air Force Institute of Technology. He earned his Ph.D. in Astronautics from Purdue University in 1970.

Following his graduation from the University of Washington, Dr. White received a commission in the U.S. Air Force. During his thirteen years of active duty he served in many capacities, including an assignment as a mission controller at Cape Kennedy during the height of the American space program. He also was an associate professor of astronautics at the Air Force Academy in Colorado for six years and has coauthored a nationally recognized textbook on astrodynamics. Dr. White resigned from active service in 1973 but continues to serve as a major general in the Air Force Reserves.

Dr. White is a registered professional engineer, a member of the Tau Beta Pi Honorary Engineering Society, and an associate fellow of the American Institute of Aeronautics and Astronautics. In 1991 and from 1993 to 1995 he served as chairman of the Colorado Rhodes Scholarship Selection Committee.

Dr. White first came into contact with The Navigators as a student at the University of Washington. Throughout his military career he maintained close contact with The Navigators, beginning the organization's ministries at the Air Force Academy and Purdue University. He served in several leadership roles with The Navigators. He became president and general director in 1986.

In addition to his work with The Navigators, Dr. White is an avid handball player, a licensed commercial pilot, and an active member of his local church, having served on the church board. He and his wife, Mary, have four children (the eldest, Steve, died in 1990), nine grandchildren, and live in Colorado Springs, Colorado.

Dr. White has written several books, including *Friends and Friendship* (with Mary). Mary is the author of *Harsh Grief, Gentle Hope* (NavPress, 1995). The following titles are available through Singapore NavPress: *On the Job: Survival or Satisfaction?* and *Making the Grade*. Contact the Castle Bookstore, Glen Eyrie Conference Center, P.O. Box 6000, Colorado Springs, CO 80934.